MW00910736

Penguin Advanced
Reading Skills

Penguin Advanced Reading Skills

Enid Nolan-Woods
David Foll

Penguin Books

Penguin Books Ltd, Harmondsworth, Middlesex, England
Viking Penguin Inc., 40 West 23rd Street, New York, New York 10010, U.S.A.
Penguin Books Australia Ltd, Ringwood, Victoria, Australia
Penguin Books Canada Limited, 2801 John Street, Markham, Ontario, Canada L3R 1B4
Penguin Books (N.Z.) Ltd, 182–190 Wairau Road, Auckland 10, New Zealand

First published 1986
Copyright © Enid Nolan-Woods and David Foll, 1986
All rights reserved

Typeset, printed and bound in Great Britain by
Hazell Watson & Viney Limited,
Member of the BPCC Group,
Aylesbury, Bucks
Typeset in Palatino

Contents

Acknowledgements

Our grateful thanks are due to the following people: Ros Milner and Chris Hudson for helping to test the material; the late Andrew Gallagher for triggering off some of the ideas; the teachers on the EFL teachers' course at the Polytechnic of Central London Summer School 1984; the many students who acted as willing guinea pigs; and last, but not least, Joy McKellen for her own very special kind of help.

E. N.-W.
D.F.

For permission to reproduce illustrations in this book, the publishers gratefully acknowledge the following: for the photograph of the South-East Asian child (p.29): Brendan Beirne; for Gainsborough, *Mr and Mrs Robert Andrews* (p. 74): the Trustees, the National Gallery, London; for the photograph of the Persian Wheel (p. 83): John and Penny Hubley; for the photograph of the balancing trough (p. 83) and the diagrams in Unit 8: Oxfam; for Foppa, Vincenzo, *The Young Cicero Reading* (p. 78): the Trustees, The Wallace Collection, London; for the photographs of the marmoset (p. 15) and the peccary (p. 18): the Zoological Society of London.

For permission to reproduce copyright material, grateful acknowledgement is made to the following: for the advertisement 'Do advertisements sometimes distort the truth?': the Advertising Standards Authority; for the extract from Procacci, Ugo, 'The technique of mural paintings and their detachment': The Hayward Gallery, London; for Hudson, R. A., *Sociolinguistics*: Cambridge University Press; for the extract from Harrison, Harry, *Make Room! Make Room!*, copyright © Harry Harrison, 1966: Doubleday & Co. Inc., and A. P. Watt & Son; for Adams, Sally, on Spender, Dale (ed.), *Man Made Language* (Routledge & Kegan Paul, 1980): the *Guardian*; for Wade Labarge, Margaret, *Medieval Travellers*: Hamish Hamilton Ltd; for the Nursing Association advertisement 'Could you have unravelled this man's mind?': the Controller, Her Majesty's Stationery Office; for the extract from Steinbeck, John, *The Grapes of Wrath*: William Heinemann Ltd; for the extract from Picard, Barbara Leone, *Hero Tales from the British Isles*: William Heinemann Ltd; for the advertisement 'Are you wanted by the police?' (in which the pay figures shown are for 1984): the Home Office; for the extract from 'Boat People Adrift in London': London's Alternative Magazine; for Pinter, Harold, *Request Stop*: Methuen Ltd; for Roth, David, *Pleasure Machine*, copyright © Omni Publications International Ltd, 1980: the copyright owner; for Mister, Robert, *What is Appropriate Technology?*: Oxfam; for Raine, Craig, 'A Martian sends a postcard home': Oxford University Press; for Berger, John, *Ways of Seeing*: Penguin Books Ltd; for Storr, Anthony, *Human Aggression*: Penguin Books Ltd; for the extracts from *Oil for Everybody*: Shell International Petroleum Co. Ltd; for the extracts from Theroux, Paul, 'The Underground Jungle': the author.

Note Extracts at the beginning of sections in the introduction all come from *Alice's Adventures in Wonderland* by Lewis Carroll.

Introduction

Who is this book for?

('You can't be a Queen, you know, till you've passed the proper examination. And the sooner we begin the better.')

This book is for more advanced students who probably have a Cambridge First Certificate in English. It is an invaluable aid to students who are studying for the Cambridge Certificate of Proficiency in English, the RSA Communicative Use of English as a Foreign Language examination (Advanced level) or the American TOEFL(500+).

It is also a book for people who want to improve their reading strategies and skills in order to read more effectively, whether for study purposes or pleasure.

What does it contain?

('What's the use of a book,' thought Alice, 'without pictures or conversations?')

This book has both pictures and conversations and much more besides. There is a wide variety of material, flexibility of form and a clear underlying structure which give an overall consistency. The varied texts require different responses, practical and creative, from the student, and are both stimulating and motivating to use.

Instruction and practice are given in a wide variety of reading strategies and skills. The nine units, exploiting areas of topical interest, each have one main focus. The units are then divided into two or three sections, each built round an authentic text.

The material is presented in a carefully graded fashion, beginning with the development of reading strategies and skills, continuing with techniques for appreciating the organization of a text and concluding with the interpretation of and response to a text.

The book is clearly laid out and easy to use, with a comprehensive contents list, an integrated reading skills analysis chart, a list of the books featured in each unit which can be used for extensive reading, a complete key and a full index.

How do you use it?

('Begin at the beginning,' the King said very gravely, 'and go on till you come to the end; then stop.')

The book has been carefully graded from easy to more difficult material and should therefore be worked through from the beginning to the end. The reading skills have been fully integrated, so it would be difficult to attempt a skimming or scanning exercise in, for example, Unit 5 if the strategies had not been understood and practised in Unit 1. At the beginning of each unit there is a clear explanation of the skill under review. Reference has been made to the use of a dictionary in certain sections; any good monolingual dictionary will do.

The material has been designed for use either in a class setting or by students individually. It is highly accessible, with clear explanations and instructions and an answer key. Anyone using it alone should read the notes to the teacher as well as those to the student.

Why do you need it?

('If there's no meaning in it,' said the King, 'that saves a world of trouble, you know, as we needn't try to find any. And yet I don't know,' he went on, spreading out the verses on his knee, and looking at them with one eye; 'I seem to see some meaning in them, after all.')

Many people find reading a difficult, slow process, yielding up very little pleasure; therefore they avoid engaging in it unless it is necessary for obtaining information or studying. Often the failure to find enjoyment and meaning in reading is caused by a lack of the necessary skills and strategies.

After working through this book, you will be able to decipher meaning in texts where originally there appeared to be none. You will have realized latent reading ability through the judicious study and practice of reading techniques. Incomprehension will give way to understanding and you will end up reading extensively with ease and enjoyment. Do not forget that reading is an *active* process. This book shows you how to activate your reading.

When do you use it?

('And how many hours a day did you do lessons?' said Alice, in a hurry to change the subject.
'Ten hours the first day,' said the Mock Turtle: 'nine the next; and so on.'
'What a curious plan!' exclaimed Alice.)

Use this book whenever you have a problem with reading. The nine units provide comprehensive coverage of the skills, strategies and approaches needed for reading English to an advanced level. After you have worked through the book, keep it by you for reference: the complete index will help you find the section you need quickly and easily; the reading skills analysis chart will show you how the skills, strategies and approaches are integrated so that you can follow the logical progression of the book; while the table of contents will give you guidance as to theme. Keep *Penguin Advanced Reading Skills* with you as your Bible, Talmud, Koran or Bhagavad-Gita.

Where does it fit in?

('Curiouser and curiouser!' cried Alice (she was so much surprised, that for a moment she quite forgot how to speak good English).)

The book can be included in any course preparatory to the Cambridge Certificate of Proficiency in English examination, the RSA CUEFL examination (Advanced level), the TOEFL (500+) or any other advanced examination. It is one of a series of skills books published by Penguin Books. Each complements the others and covers one of the four language skills of reading, writing, speaking and listening.

Notes to the teacher

The book is aimed at students with an advanced level of English and teaches reading techniques. Many students find reading a difficult process but do not know how to improve their reading ability; we hope that this book will help them to do so and also to gain pleasure from reading. We have included coverage of the following wide range of reading skills, strategies and approaches to reading, together with copious practice material:

previewing	word use
anticipation	text analysis
skimming and scanning	visual classification
prediction	interpretation
close reading	extraction of information
inference	evaluation of the text

How to use the book

The book is progressively graded so it is advisable to work through it unit by unit. Clear contents listing, a comprehensive index and an integrated reading skills analysis chart make the material easy to find and use.

Each of the units is divided into two or three sections based on individual reading texts. Within the sections there are five or six activities employing a variety of exercises designed to take the student through a logical progression of skills, strategies and approaches to reading. Each unit has been designed to cover comprehensively the targeted skill or technique, but teachers wishing to exploit the material further can do so by working on detailed vocabulary in the text, further comprehension and discussion. For the weaker student this is best done in a pair or group. Clear instructions and guidance have been given in the units on how to use the material. All of the language skills are interactive, so speaking, listening or writing can all be incorporated in a reading programme. This book is concerned with developing the reading skills, but there are sister volumes which concentrate on the other skills which could be used alongside this book.

Notes to the student

The material is aimed at an advanced level. It has been devised to extend your reading abilities and to help you enjoy reading.

There is an interesting range of texts, both factual and imaginative, which have been carefully selected from a variety of sources with the aim of providing maximum interest: novels, plays, poems, newspapers and magazines, journals, advertisements, modern fiction and legends.

A wide range of reading skills, strategies and techniques has been covered, drawn from contemporary work in this field. The material is thoroughly taught, not just tested, and there is a large variety of exercises with which you can practise. We hope you will find these both motivating and stimulating; we have, we think, presented them in a lively, integrated and interesting way.

The book can be used by you alone (there is a full key at the back of the book) or with a class. If you are studying in a class then you will be able to extend your reading skills through pair and group work, role play and discussion as well as through individual work. Whichever way you are working, though, there are clear instructions, a skills analysis chart, a contents list, an index and a relevant reading list to help you in your study. Good luck and enjoy yourself.

Integrated reading skills analysis chart

Unit 1
Animals

Section A

Skimming:
content
text-type
function
tone
Scanning

Section B

Skimming:
content
function
tone
Scanning

Section C

Skimming:
content 1
Skimming:
content 2

Unit 2
Community

Section A

Previewing:
titles and
headings
blurbs
table of
contents
illustrations

Section B

Prediction:
ends of
sentences

Anticipation
Close reading
Scanning
Close reading
Word use:
synonyms

Prediction:
continuation of
a story

Anticipation
Evaluation of
the text

Unit 3
Travel

Section A

Anticipation
Skimming:
text-type
Prediction
Scanning
Close reading

Inference:
unfamiliar
words

Section B

Skimming:
text-type

Inference:
unfamiliar
words
implied
meaning

Word use:
synonyms
Evaluation of
the text

Unit 4
Language

Section A

Anticipation
Skimming:
function
text-type
content
Prediction
Close reading
Inference:
unfamiliar words
Word use:
lexical sets

Cohesion:
reference
ellipsis

Summary
Evaluation of
the text
Extraction of
information

Section B

Anticipation
Skimming:
content
Scanning
Word use:
definitions
Close reading

Cohesion:
discourse
markers

Evaluation of
the text

Unit 5
Advertising

Section A

Skimming:
content
Scanning
Inference:
unfamiliar words
Word use:
varieties of
meaning

Text analysis 1:
discourse at
sentence
level

Style
Extraction of
information
Evaluation of
the text

Section B

Anticipation
Close reading
Inference:
unfamiliar words

Text analysis 1:
discourse at
paragraph
level

Style
Evaluation of
the text

Section C

Anticipation
Skimming:
content
Scanning
Inference:
unfamiliar words
Word use:
antonyms
word-play
Style

Text analysis 1:
discourse at
whole-text
level

Evaluation of
the text

Unit 6
Psychology

Section A

Anticipation
Skimming:
  content
  text-type
  function
  tone
Close reading
Word use:
  equivalents
Cohesion:
  reference
  ellipsis

Text analysis 2:
  cause and
  effect

Summary
Evaluation of
  the text

Section B

Anticipation
Skimming:
  content
Scanning
Word use:
  synonyms

Text analysis 2:
  contrast

Summary

Section C

Prediction
Close reading
Inference:
  implied meaning

Text analysis 2:
  comparison

Evaluation of
  the text

Unit 7
Art

Section A

Anticipation
Skimming:
  function
  text-type
Scanning
Close reading
Word use:
  dictionary use
Inference:
  unfamiliar words

Visual
  comprehension:
  picture
  response

Section B

Anticipation
Close reading
Word use:
  definitions
  antonyms
  equivalents
Close reading
Inference:
  implied meaning

Visual
  comprehension:
  text response

Unit 8
Technology

Section A

Anticipation
Scanning

Visual
  classification:
  illustration to
  support a
  text

Inference:
  unfamiliar words
Close reading
Inference:
  unfamiliar words
Word use:
  definitions
  synonyms
Extraction of
  information
Evaluation of
  the text

Section B

Prediction
Skimming:
  content
Labelling a
diagram

Visual
  classification:
  illustrations
  to clarify
  instructions

Section C

Anticipation
Skimming:
  content
Word use:
  word building

Visual
  classification:
  diagrams

Summary
Close reading

Unit 9
Literature

Section A

Anticipation
Close reading
Cohesion:
  discourse
  markers
  reference

Interpretation

Evaluation of
  the text

Section B

Prediction
Scanning
Close reading
Word use:
  equivalents

Interpretation

Anticipation
Prediction

Interpretation

Evaluation of
  the text

Section C

Skimming:
  content
Close reading

Interpretation

Evaluation of
  the text

Unit 1 **Animals**

Skimming and scanning

Both skimming and scanning are useful reading skills that may at first seem strange to a learner who is used to reading everything in a foreign language with the same degree of attention and care. Both skills require you to jump through the text, ignoring parts of it: you may be looking quickly over the text to get a general, superficial idea of the content (and there may or may not be a reason for a subsequent, more careful reading) – this we call **skimming**; or you may be looking quickly through the text searching for a specific piece of information or to see if the text is suitable for a specific reading purpose – this we call **scanning**.

Skimming

Ask yourself, 'What is this text about?' Move your eyes quickly over the text, looking especially at the titles, the beginning and end, and the first sentence of every paragraph (where the more important information is often placed).

Scanning

Ask yourself, 'Has this text got what I'm looking for and, if so, where is it?' Move your eyes quickly over the text on the look-out for specific items (e.g. names or dates).

Section A

Skimming for content

First you are going to practise skimming to get a general idea of content. This is what you do:

1   Look at the headings and headlines a–o on pages 12 and 13, then turn to page 14.

a HMV demands an end to dog label parody

By Our Arts Correspondent

b Activity Books: Bird Watching. By G. Thomas Franklin Watts, £3.50, 085166 9980

c Watch the wooden birdie!

d PRINCE RESIGNS OVER HIPPO MENU

e LEARN TO LIVE WITH

f   **Waiting in the wings**

g   <u>LOST</u>

PLEASE HELP

ℓ **NEWTS PREVENT HOUSE BUILDING**

m

h # British Deer Society

Patron: His Royal Highness The Prince of Wales,
K.G., K.T., G.C.B., A.D.C.(P.)

MEMBERSHIP FORM

i **Dog's shopping cart 'illegal'**

j ## Making the mussels do it elsewhere

k **Prehistoric foal footprints found**

n MARMOSETS

o ## The fund in action

YOUR NEIGHBOURS.

2 Look quickly over texts 1–15 on pages 14–16 and match them with the correct headings or headlines. Do this as quickly as possible. Do not try to read through each text carefully.

1

TRANSATLANTIC literary folk who, in the James Thurber-Dorothy Parker tradition, head for the Algonquin Hotel when they are in New York, will relish the news that "Hamlet III" is being primed in the wings for the feline world's role of a lifetime.

The first Hamlet, a snooty cat and sometimes a biter, was the lord of the Algonquin lobby for 14 years. He pioneered the hotel's tradition of having an orange cat slink through the lobby with such distinction that he was immortalised in a book "Algonquin Cat." On his death two years ago, VARIETY, the show business weekly, ran his obituary.

Hamlet II, a gift from a New Yorker, was a beauty who, alas, had a brief reign. When he disappeared last spring it was widely suspected that he had eloped with his girlfriend at the neighbouring New York Yacht Club.

The hotel is bringing Hamlet III along in slow stages, anxious to avoid a disappointment. But I hear that his debut is due soon.

4

ANOTHER book to use along with various bird identification guides. Here is a wide-ranging collection of field projects and activities working from the familiar – feeding garden birds, collecting owl pellets and making a bird census – to the less familiar – plotting territories, measuring the speed of flight, timing birds diving and making a sparrow dust box. There is lots more besides to occupy and entertain the young bird watcher. A valuable project book to introduce to your students.

2

Mr Mike Carter, a carpenter, of Yate, near Bristol, has been told that he may be prosecuted if he continues to let his dog take groceries home in a specially-built cart.

The RSPCA says that using the cart breaks the 1911 Protection of Animals Act.

3

Mr King, Environment secretary, has refused to support developers who were seeking planning permission to build a housing estate on a breeding site for the rare Great Crested newt at Cawood, near Selby, North Yorks.

He dismissed an appeal by the builders against Selby District Council's original refusal

5

(Eaten in a year)
400 million chickens
16 million turkeys
14.5 million pigs
13.9 million sheep
4.2 million cattle
802,946 tons seafish
7,600 tons farmed fish
12.8 billion pints of milk
13.2 billion eggs
773,000 tons cheese and butter

EXPORTS
9.6 million chickens
15,925 pigeons
5,800 horses

SCIENTISTS working for Shell believe they have come up with a cost-effective way of stopping over-sexed mussels from undermining our North Sea oil industry, *writes John Huxley.*

Last week The Sunday Times described how offshore operators had virtually despaired of preventing a build-up of multiplying molluscs on the legs of oil rigs. This week, Shell researchers will unveil its answer: non-toxic, anti-fouling compound which exudes a thin film of oil. When the mass of mussels becomes heavy or "becomes agitated in any other way, such as wave action," they simply fall off.

Meanwhile, Sunday Times readers have written in with their own ingenious suggestion for getting the industry out of its multi-million pound scrape. One suggested building diversionary decoy rigs alongside the real things.

Yet another reader advises that the sex life of the marauding mussels should be dampened in the time-honoured way: by administration of a bucket of cold water. The Great Debate continues.

7

Lifespan: 12 years
Height: 6 to 12in
Weight: 5 to 12oz
Price: from £150

Native to South and Central America, where they occupy the forest's high canopy, feeding on fruit, insects and eggs. They are about the size of a squirrel, with long, grasping tails and clawed feet. They live in family groups of three to eight, with the father taking major responsibility for the young once they are weaned.

Capable of producing two pairs of offspring a year, they are therefore increasingly favoured by researchers. About 50 per cent now come from domestic breeding sources. Used primarily for reproduction and fertility studies, also behavioural, psychological, bacteriological and pharmacological work.

8

EMI Records is preparing to go to court over Nipper, the dog on the His Master's Voice record label.

It has been angered by an independent record company Dead Dog Records, which parodies the HMV label.

EMI says that the Dead Dog label will imply a connexion between the two companies and has threatened legal action unless it is withdrawn within 14 days.

"The validity and reputation of this trade mark are of the utmost importance and, for many years, we have actively protected the reputation of this mark and have taken determined action to protest about and to act against its unauthorized use".

Mr John Clare, a director of Dead Dog Records, said: "It is not our intention to cause any confusion between the two companies, but we have grown quite attached to our dead dog and would prefer not to lose him".

The original painting which hangs in EMI headquarters, is the work of Francis Barraud, who portrayed his dog Nipper gazing into a gramophone horn.

9

THESE replica puffins, photographed here above a cliff in West Wales, are to be erected on Cardigan Island, off the north Pembrokeshire coast, as a lure for the real thing.
The original puffin population was wiped out 50 years ago by rats which came ashore from a shipwreck, and they have never returned. The hope is that the sham birds will attract passing puffins into landing then excavate nesting burrows.
Ornithologist Peter Davies, of the West Wales Naturalists Trust, decided to try the scheme, after the success of American 'lures.' There will be no danger from rats. They have all been exterminated.

10

If you're fascinated by BBC Wildlife programmes, then you'll be enthralled by *BBC Wildlife:* the monthly colour magazine produced in co-operation with our natural history unit.

Featuring the talents of the world's key wildlife and conservation experts, top photographers and well-known broadcasting personalities, the magazine will be enjoyed by the professional and enthusiast alike.

There's something for all the family.

As well as the monthly articles illustrated in full colour, there are regular features that include wildlife questions, television and book reviews, exclusive monthly listings of programmes, quizzes and an international news section that brings you news of the latest discoveries.

BBC WILDLIFE £1 PLACE AN ORDER WITH YOUR NEWSAGENT AND EXPLORE THE WORLD OF NATURE FROM THE COMFORT OF YOUR OWN ARMCHAIR.

11

on Wednesday night
" POLLY "
red and white Welsh
Springer Spaniel
Please ring:
602.7453
or 739.8262
(answerphone)

12

If you care for deer join a young, enthusiastic and rapidly growing society and so help preserve part of our national heritage.

The British Deer Society welcomes to its membership all those who value the British countryside and its wildlife, who regard deer as part of its heritage, and who would be glad to join with others in safeguarding that heritage.

13

Prince Philip has resigned from the New York based Explorers' Club because he was "appalled" because hippopotamus steaks and lion meat were served at its annual dinner last year, Buckingham Palace said last night.

The Prince, a member of the World Wildlife Fund, did not attend the annual dinner with its bizarre menu. But he wrote to the club saying he was "appalled by the exhibition of bad taste." The Aga Khan also resigned.

14

Fossil footprints of *Hipparion*, forerunner of the horse, made 3.5 million years ago, have been found in Tanzania.

An analysis at the State University, Utrecht, Netherlands, has revealed a *Hipparion* foal accompanied by two adults on a slippery, soft volcanic ash surface.

15

The World Wildlife Fund was established in 1961 to help to stop man's destruction of the natural environment on which all human, animal and plant life depends.

Such well-known conservationists as HRH Duke of Edinburgh, Sir Peter Scott and David Attenborough are closely associated with our work.

In 21 short years, WWF has raised and spent over £30 million on nearly 3,000 projects. Its activities are many and varied.

Skimming for text-type, function and tone

Now skim each text and consider it from three points of view:
  i where has the text come from and what sort of text is it? (text-type)
 ii what is the intention of the text? (function)
iii what is the tone of the text? (tone)
Using the lists below, draw up a profile for each text. One example has been done for you. Again, do this as quickly as possible. Try to make your decisions on a general, not detailed, understanding of the text.

Example:	text-type	function	tone
2	a	b	a

text-type
a a newspaper article
b an advertisement
c a notice
d a book review
e publicity material
f an extract from a textbook
g an extract from an encyclopaedia

function
a to review and recommend
b to report news
c to advertise and persuade
d to give a description
e to request something
f to tell an amusing story
g to publicize
h to give information

tone
a neutral
b half-neutral/half-humorous
c supportive

Scanning

Now you are going to practise scanning to find specific pieces of information. Find the answers to these questions as quickly as possible. Do not read more than is necessary to provide the answer.

1 What is the name of the New York-based club Prince Philip has resigned from?
2 How much is a copy of *BBC Wildlife*?
3 What is the name of the record company EMI Records is preparing to take to court?
4 When was Polly lost?
5 What are the cats at the Algonquin Hotel traditionally called?
6 How many million chickens a year do the British eat?
7 Why are mussels worrying the offshore oil industry?
8 Who or what is *Hipparion*?
9 What animal prevented a housing estate being built?
10 In what year was the Protection of Animals Act passed?
11 Why are marmosets so popular with laboratory researchers?
12 Why is it safe for puffins to come back and nest on Cardigan Island?
13 When was the World Wildlife Fund established?
14 Who is the patron of the British Deer Society?
15 What is the name of the publishers of the book *Bird Watching*?

Section B

Skimming

These are the beginnings and endings of two newspaper articles that appeared in the *Observer* on successive Sundays.

1 Can you establish the content, function and tone of each article from the extracts given? Discuss your answers. Use the categories on p.17 to help you.

NOT WANTED

The collared peccary, a South American creature which is described as a cross between a rat and a pig, has emerged as the most unloved animal in Whipsnade Park Zoo.

The unpopularity of the peccary has long been suspected. Now the zoo's animal adoption scheme, under which members of the public 'adopt' animals, has confirmed it. No one wants a peccary.

Mrs Anne Mead, the zoo's adoption officer, said: 'Unfortunately they are ugly, smelly animals. As far as adoption is concerned, they seem to be a complete non-starter.'

Unlovely but loved

by PETER CHIPPINDALE

The collared peccaries (above), previously the most unloved animals in Whipsnade Park Zoo, spent last week basking in a surge of affection from the British public.

After exposure of the peccaries' plight in *The Observer*, last week, the zoo was inundated with press and TV cameras and letters and telephone calls from people all over the country.

'Previously they used to stand stock-still or run away when people inspected them closely, but now they seem to have lost a lot of their nerves and have been quite frisky.'

2 Tick as many answers as you think correct.

i The first article
   a ☐ expresses surprise that no one has adopted the peccaries.
   b ☐ describes the peccaries in flattering terms.
   c ☐ makes it clear why no one has adopted the peccaries.

ii The second article says that
   a ☐ the paper was responsible for drawing the public's attention to the peccaries.
   b ☐ lots of people gave reasons for not wanting to adopt the peccaries.
   c ☐ the peccaries have become overnight stars as a result of the first article.

3 Put paragraphs a, b and c back in the correct place. Read each one and decide
   if it belongs to the first or second article.

a
> 'That's all changed now,' Mrs
> Anne Mead, the zoo's animal
> adoption officer, said yesterday.
> 'We have never had such a
> response, even to the birth of the
> baby black rhino last year.'

c
> *The Observer* revealed how the
> zoo's animal adoption scheme,
> under which people adopt animals
> and help to pay the cost of their
> upkeep, had confirmed the long-
> suspected unpopularity of the pec-
> caries. Nobody wanted to adopt
> one.

b
> Apart from being ugly, they are
> extremely boring, squelching back-
> wards and forwards on little
> stumpy legs in their enclosure
> which they have turned into a sea
> of mud. They can be vicious, chat-
> tering their teeth like machine-
> guns when cornered, and are cap-
> able of inflicting a nasty bite.

Scanning

Read these questions first, and then find the answers as quickly as possible in
the two newspaper articles.

1 Which zoo do these peccaries live in?
2 Which newspaper published the story of the peccaries?
3 Where do peccaries come from?
4 What is the name of the zoo's animal adoption officer?

Section C

Skimming for content 1

Here are the first sentences from the main sections of a leaflet advertising the
Adopt an Animal Scheme at London Zoo. You should be able to get a quick idea
of the whole leaflet by reading just these first sentences (extracts 1–5).

1 Read quickly extracts 1–5.

1 ADOPT AN ANIMAL
*From now on your visits to London Zoo can be even more exciting and worthwhile.
Because this is your chance not only to see one of the largest collections of
wild animals in the world, **but to visit your very own animal.***

2 WHY YOU SHOULD THINK ABOUT ADOPTING
*London Zoo is one of the most famous zoos in the world, and, along with
Whipsnade Zoo forms our National Zoological Collection.*

3 HOW THE ADOPT AN ANIMAL SCHEME WORKS
*The Scheme is based on what it costs to keep and feed an animal for one year,
broken down into adoption units of £30.*

4   WHAT YOU GET

£30 Adoption Units:
When you become an adopter you'll receive an Adoption Certificate, a photograph of the animal you've adopted, a complimentary entrance ticket or a reduced price season ticket (a free Group Season Ticket for group adopters) and your name will appear on a special plaque on or near the animal's enclosure.

5   HOW TO BECOME AN ADOPTER

Simply choose your animal (if the animal that you choose is not available because all the units have already been taken up, the Adopt an Animal Office will suggest other possibilities), complete the enclosed application form, and either hand it in at London Zoo's main offices or post it to the address given on the form.

2   From reading extracts 1–5 can you guess the content of the rest of each extract? Which of the choices a, b, c or d best expresses the idea already conceived in each extract? (Note that the question numbers relate to the extract numbers.)

1a London Zoo has one of the best collections of animals in the world.
 b London Zoo has more than 8,000 animals.
 c There is an animal for everyone.
 d You can adopt any of the animals in the zoo.

2a Adoption is now one of the most popular ways of raising money for the zoo.
 b We need your help to maintain our collection.
 c The scheme is based on what it costs to keep an animal for one year.
 d If you pay the full cost, we will put up your name next to the cage.

3a Simply choose your animal and fill in the form.
 b You will receive an Adoption Certificate and a free ticket.
 c An elephant costs 170 units, but small animals cost only £10.
 d You can make your visit more enjoyable by visiting your own animal.

4a You will also receive a copy of an animal newsletter.
 b London Zoo is a registered charity and relies on your help.
 c An adoption would make a very special present for someone.
 d Our Adopt an Animal Scheme is open to any group or individual.

5 How do you think extract 5 was completed in the original leaflet? With:
 a a certificate?
 b a form?
 c a photograph?
 d a ticket?

Skimming for content 2

On page 21 are the first sentences of each paragraph of a newspaper article. Reading these should be enough to enable you to get a general idea of the content of the whole article.

1 Read sentences 1–7. Then evaluate statements a–t according to this scale:

Y=Yes L=Likely P=Possible U=Unlikely N=No DK=Don't Know

1 THE LAST MOUSE in Dr John Calhoun's experimental universe died a few weeks ago, exactly four years and six months after Dr Calhoun had created what he thought was an ideal world for mice at the National Institute for Mental Health in Poolesville, Maryland.

a The mice were unable to live in this Utopia.

b The mice died of a mystery virus attack.

2 In theory this ideal world could accommodate 4,000 mice and there was enough food and water for many more.

c The maximum population of the colony was more than 4,000 mice.

d In the first year the population grew from four pairs to 1,000 mice.

e Many mice lived to the equivalent of eighty human years.

3 Then breeding began to slow down.

f The young males could not establish a territory of their own.

g There were large numbers of unattached males.

h The females began to eat their babies.

i The unattached males disturbed the breeding females.

4 As a result the baby mice were prematurely rejected by their mothers and started life without having developed normal social and emotional bonds.

j These mice never developed normal courtship and breeding behaviour.

k Many males devoted all their attention to themselves.

l There was a high incidence of homosexuality.

5 As the old generation of potent mice gradually died off they were replaced at an ever decreasing rate by the impotent beautiful ones and their female counterparts.

m Even when put in separate cages with normal mice they were unable to breed adequately.

n The number of mice in the colony continued to rise.

6 The final extinction of the colony would not have been predicted by most biologists.

o There was a catastrophic breakdown in social organization in the mice Utopia.

p Biologists expected the number of mice to undergo periodic fluctuations.

q The problems arose because mortality rates were artificially reduced.

r Mammals survive better in a hostile environment.

7 Dr Calhoun sees in his experiment an allegory of human life on planet Earth.

s Dr Calhoun thinks a human Utopia is achievable.

t Dr Calhoun predicts a similar catastrophe for mankind.

2 Now read the complete article. How much were you able to understand from the first sentence of each paragraph?

Death in paradise

THE LAST MOUSE in Dr John Calhoun's experimental universe died a few weeks ago, exactly four years and six months after Dr Calhoun had created what he thought was an ideal world for mice at the National Institute for Mental Health in Poolesville, Maryland. In Universe 25, which Dr Calhoun says he created as a Utopia for mice, they appeared to have everything they could possibly want—plenty of food and water, warmth, freedom from disease and space to exercise. But the mice were unable to live happily together in their man-made universe and so the colony was doomed.

In theory this ideal world could accommodate 4,000 mice and there was enough food and water for many more. The first four pairs to colonise this universe soon grew to like it and within a year there were a thousand mice. Many of these mice lived to the ripe old age of 800 days—equivalent to 80 years in human terms.

Then breeding began to slow down. The young males were unable to establish a territory of their own and gathered together fighting and moping in the centre of the floor. These young mugger mice made random senseless attacks on each other and became covered in wounds and scars. The young females on the other hand withdrew to the high nesting boxes which had been left in a convenient spot for breeding. The large numbers of unattached young mice began to make it difficult for the others to breed. They invaded the nests and disturbed the breeding females.

As a result the baby mice were prematurely rejected by their mothers and started life without having developed normal social and emotional bonds. This generation of young mice was not aggressive like the muggers. They were withdrawn and never developed normal courtship and breeding behaviour. Dr Calhoun called these males " the beautiful ones " because they never fought and so their fur was always in good condition. They ate, drank, slept and groomed themselves but took no part in social or sexual activities.

As the old generation of potent mice gradually died off they were replaced at an ever decreasing rate by the impotent beautiful ones and their female counterparts. Even when some of these mice were taken out of their utopia and put into separate cages with normal mice of the opposite sex they were unable to breed adequately.

The final extinction of the colony would not have been predicted by most biologists. The colony could have been expected to grow up again from a few remnant breeding groups and go through periodic cycles of large and small numbers. Dr Calhoun believes that the catastrophic breakdown in social organisation which spelt the death of Universe 25 could happen in any species of mammal where mortality is reduced artificially. It could happen in human communities when modern medicine allows the prolonged survival of older people and there is not enough suitable accommodation in which young people can safely and securely raise their families.

Dr Calhoun sees in his experiment an allegory of human life on planet Earth. He foresees the possibility of a similar fate for man and expresses it in apocalyptic terms.

Unit 2 **Community**

Previewing and prediction

Before approaching a text, a great deal of information about it can be obtained by **previewing,** i.e. by considering the clues given in the title, the blurb (the information on the back of the book or on the inside covers), the table of contents, the index and any illustrations. Further information can be obtained from prefaces, introductions, bibliographies or even acknowledgements.

One of the most important reading skills is **prediction**, anticipating what is to come next in a text. We all have certain expectations about any material that we choose to read, and there are various clues to help us predict the probable nature of the subject matter and its development and treatment.

Previewing

In the first part of the unit some of the previewing skills are practised, using titles, blurbs, a table of contents and illustrations.

Prediction

In the second part you also learn to make use of the skill of prediction by asking yourself: How will the writer end this sentence or paragraph? What do I expect to come next? How will the story continue? How will it end?

Section A

Previewing using titles and headings

The title, or heading, is often the most obvious clue to what is to follow. But be careful, as it can be misleading.

1   Look at the following titles or headings and write down what you think is the likely content of each book or article.

a **Blueprint for Greentown?**

b Love's Real Estate

c If it wasn't for the jokes

d **Boat People Adrift in London**

e *On the road with scrap and straw*

f **The Grapes of Wrath**

g **Our Troubled Kids**

h **Convoy to Nowhere**

For which title is it easiest to suggest a subject? For which is it hardest?

2   Here is a list of the actual subjects of each of the books or articles. See if you can match them with the titles or headings. The first has been done for you.
1   A caring religious community b
2   Vietnamese refugees who arrived by sea
3   The gipsy way of life
4   A modern hippie commune that's lost its way
5   An ecological community for the future
6   Community help for juveniles
7   Humour in the language of miners
8   A dispossessed community fruit-picking in California
How accurate were your first suggestions?

3   Which of the following articles or books would you consult if you were study-ing the effects of new technology on community life? Consider the subtitles as well as the main titles and headings.

a *Lost generation*
Unemployed youth

b Automation for the Office Worker
How does it affect you?

c **Conflict, Change and our Future**
Issues of conflict and change in children

d The Industrialization Process
Mechanization and society

e The World in a City
The multi-cultural society

f **NEW TECHNOLOGY**
Job content and grading

g *Family and work in rural societies*
Perspectives on wage and non-wage labour

h COMMUNITY RELATIONS
Today - and Tomorrow?

Give reasons for your choice.

Previewing using blurbs
Match the blurbs on pages 26–27 with these titles:

a My Part of the River

b *Ash on a Young Man's Sleeve*

c MAKE ROOM! MAKE ROOM!

d The Last Frontier

e A CHILD IN THE FOREST

f THE HITCH-HIKER'S GUIDE TO THE GALAXY

g STILL GLIDES THE STREAM

h A HOUSE OF LIONS

1

'People of Earth, your attention please. This is Prosetnic Vogon Jeltz of the Galactic Hyperspace Planning Council.

Plans for development of the outlying regions of the galaxy require the building of a hyperspatial express route through your star system, and regrettably your planet is scheduled for demolition.

The progress will take slightly less than two of your Earth minutes. Thank you'

For Arthur Dent, earthling and homeowner, the severe case of planning blight announced above is the overture to a quite remarkable set of travels, guided en route by an equally remarkable book — a book more popular than the **Celestial Home Care Omnibus,** cheaper than the **Encyclopedia Galactica,** it's . . .

2

'A winner . . . a vivid and personal story of the life and hardships faced by a Forest of Dean miner's family in the 1920s . . . a moving commentary on the Forest way of life as seen through the eyes of a child'
GLOUCESTERSHIRE LIFE

'A land of oak and fern, of secret hill farms and plain, matter-of-fact market towns . . . Still a Forester, Winifred Foley recalls vividly but unsentimentally the loving, poverty-stricken home where she was brought up'
BIRMINGHAM POST

'Warm-hearted and well-observed'
SUNDAY TELEGRAPH

'The story is funny and touching by turns'
MANCHESTER EVENING NEWS

5

'In Bloomsbury, there are nine characters in search of an author'

A group of rational and liberal individuals, characterized by intelligence, charm and a hard work ethic, or dangerous animals, rather suspicious of each other? Who and what were the Bloomsburys?

Pulitzer Prize-winner and world-renowned for his biography of Henry James, Leon Edel has brought his enormous talents to bear in this elegant, vivid, beautifully ironic and completely assured introduction to such figures as Virginia Woolf, Duncan Grant, Maynard Keynes, Roger Fry and Vanessa Bell.

'A perfect gem of style and precision' –
Louis Auchincloss

'Leon Edel has brought into strong, unified narrative all the complicated lives – hilarious, eccentric and often tragic – of these gifted and inexorable individualists . . . admirable' –
Paul Horgan

'I am overwhelmed by the beauty of this book' –
Nigel Nicolson

6

'Acutely remembered, imaginatively told . . . a clever, moving evocation' – Angus Wilson in the *Observer*

Sharp, sad and romantic, Dannie Abse's reminiscences weave the private fortunes of a Jewish family in Cardiff into the troubled tapestry of the times. Unemployment, the rise of Hitler and Mussolini, the Spanish Civil War, the fate of the European Jews; all these themes are the more real for being seen through the angry, irreverent eyes of youth – just as the neighbour's drinking problem, the Cardiff boy who died in Spain, the Reverent Aaronowich and his estranged son, seen through the same eyes, achieve universality.

'Funny, moving and idiosyncratic. Mr Abse works with poetic economy' – *New Statesman*

'An unnerving use of words which trap the imaginative reality of childhood and adolescence' – *Tribune*

3

Some seventy years ago a remnant of the tribe of Cheyenne Indians, three hundred men, women, and children, broke out of the established Indian Territory in an apparently hopeless attempt to cover the vast distance to their home in the Black Hills of Wyoming. The country they had to cross was laced – for this was in the 1870's – with new railroads and telegraph lines; it was filled with towns and homesteads. Ten thousand soldiers were sent out to stop them. But by ruse, by their lore of the wilds, by sheer refusal to be beaten, a small number eventually reached their goal.

This gallant excursion is something that could only have happened in America, and the story is as truly representative of American history as many more widely-remembered episodes.

4

1999 – automation, total welfare, and weekends on the moon . . . or an overcrowded world that knows that the dawn of the new century is the edge of disaster – a world of starving billions living on lentils, soya beans and – if they're lucky – the odd starving rat.

In a city of thirty-five million people Andy Rusch is engaged in a desperate and lonely hunt for a killer everyone has forgotten . . . for even in a world such as this a policeman can find himself utterly alone . . .

7

'The experience which fertilized Flora Thompson's imagination was a personal one – the vanished life of the countryside which she had known as a child in the eighteen-eighties and nineties . . . Her work must be taken in great draughts, and then the effect is very nearly magical. It's as though one had absorbed her experience oneself and remembered what she remembered; and knew what songs the old men sang in the inn of an evening; and what games the children played who had no toys, and never heard of a wireless or a cinema; and what were the flowers that went into a May garland . . .' *From a radio broadcast by Margaret Lane.*

'This is a book that would be worth reading for its descriptions alone . . .'
Manchester Guardian

'. . . reading it is a perfect pleasure.'
Benny Green, *Spectator*

'Which of us would not return to Restharrow if we could? Seat yourself on Miss Charity Finch's magic carpet and the thing is done.'
Punch

8

"I was born in a tenement flat in the East End of London in the year in which Queen Victoria died . . . I shall try to tell you what life was like to live so close to the Thames and its docks. Some of what I shall write about will be almost unbelievable to those who have lived only in this affluent age."

'Extraordinary warmth and hope comes through her narrative.'
THE EVENING STANDARD

'Fulfils every one of my requirements for a perfect present. I can't think of anyone who would not enjoy it and be moved by it.'
BOOKS AND BOOKMEN

Which blurb is most informative? Should a blurb tell you more about the content of a book? Who do you think writes the blurb and for what purpose?

Previewing using a table of contents

You have been asked to read a book with the title *Downwave*. What do you think it might be about?

Now look at the chapter headings in the table of contents. Do they suggest something similar? If not, what do you think now is the subject of the book? How much did the headings cause you to re-evaluate your idea? What else in the contents can help you find out about the subject? On which pages would you look?

CONTENTS

Previewing using illustrations

As well as the kinds of text considered so far, illustrations can provide an indication as to the content of a book or article.

1 What do you think the text is about that accompanies this photograph?
2 Suggest a title.
3 What kind of text do you think it is?
   a literary
   b scientific
   c romantic
   d factual

Section B

Prediction: the ends of sentences

When part of a sentence is given and you are asked to predict how it continues, you should apply two strategies:

a Take the meaning in the first part of the sentence and consider the writer's line of thought.

b Look at the vocabulary and structures in the first part of the sentence and decide what types of words are likely to follow.

For example:

The Vietnamese who have been settled in Britain have been subjected to a combination of problems which . . .

First, we can imagine that the writer saw a combination of problems bring about some difficulty in the lives of the Vietnamese.

Secondly, we can look at the vocabulary in the sentence and see that the last word is a relative pronoun and is therefore likely to be followed by a verb. Looking at the verbs in the sentence we see that they are in a perfect tense, so we can predict that the verb we need to use will also be in a perfect tense.

Applying all this information we can predict that the sentence might end:

. . . have caused some difficulty in their lives.

or

. . . have made their lives difficult.

or

. . . have made life difficult for them.

Here is part of the article which accompanies the illustration on page 29. See if you can finish the rest of the incomplete sentences using the prediction strategies suggested above. Do not look at page 31.

The Vietnamese who have been settled in Britain have been subjected to a combination of problems which . . .[1] Coming from a homeland which has suffered for decades from war and speaking little or no English, they have arrived in a country where there is virtually no established Vietnamese community to which . . .[2]

Britain's last two groups of refugees were the Hungarians in 1956 and the Ugandan Asians in the early 70's. Both of these were helped by existing communities of their own kind, who could help with . . .[3] The Vietnamese have no one except the refugee agencies, as they are not accepted by the existing Chinese community in Britain who are mostly from . . .[4]

The British Council for Aid to Refugees (BCAR), Refugee Action and the Ockenden Venture are all trying to . . .[5] BCAR has the main responsibility, but the Home Office plan to scale down their financing in the hope the local authorities will . . .[6] "Since the cut-backs in financing we are so short-staffed we can only . . .,"[7] claims Jane Thomas of BCAR. "The refugees have mostly settled in inner city areas where . . .[8] Many of them are from rural areas in Vietnam and they end up in areas like Lewisham, Southwark or Tower Hamlets. It is very hard for them to adapt, many of them are finding it very hard to learn English, they are not used to formal education and thus . . .[9]," she said.

For most of the refugees, their inability to learn English and subsequent unemployment keeps them . . .[10] The areas they have been plonked in have . . .[11]

Here is the complete article. Read it and check the accuracy of your predictions. Do not worry if you did not produce exactly the same words, but see how closely you predicted the way the writer was thinking and organizing his language.

Boat People Adrift in London

The Vietnamese who have been settled in Britain have been subjected to a combination of problems which have made life difficult for them. Coming from a homeland which has suffered for decades from war and speaking little or no English, they have arrived in a country where there is virtually no established Vietnamese community to which they could turn for support.

Britain's last two groups of refugees were the Hungarians in 1956 and the Ugandan Asians in the early 70's. Both of these were helped by existing communities of their own kind, who could help with housing, employment and social pressures. The Vietnamese have no one except the refugee agencies, as they are not accepted by the existing Chinese community in Britain who are mostly from Singapore and Hong Kong.

The British Council for Aid to Refugees (BCAR), Refugee Action and the Ockenden Venture are all trying to help the "boat people". BCAR has the main responsibility, but the Home Office plan to scale down their financing in the hope the local authorities will take increasing responsibility for the refugees. "Since the cutbacks in financing we are so short staffed we can only deal with crises," claims Jane Thomas of BCAR. "The refugees have mostly settled in inner city areas where the flats are hard to get. Many of them are from rural areas in Vietnam and they end up in areas like Lewisham, Southwark, or Tower Hamlets. It is very hard for them to adapt, many of them are finding it very hard to learn English, they are not used to formal education and thus they are finding work hard to come by," she said.

For most of the refugees, their inability to learn English and subsequent unemployment keeps them isolated and dependent. The areas they have been plonked in have few jobs available anyway.

Anticipation

The following extract is from a book, *The Grapes of Wrath*, about migrant workers in America in the 1920s. Before you look at the text, tick any of the statements that you expect to relate to the migrants.

a They were unhappy about leaving their homes. ☐
b There was very little community feeling among them. ☐
c They changed their lifestyle easily. ☐
d They looked forward to a better life in a new place. ☐
e They felt secure as they travelled around the country. ☐

Now read the extract quickly and see if your expectations are confirmed.

> Thus they changed their social life – changed as in the whole universe only man can change. They were not farm men any more, but migrant men. And the thought, the planning, the long staring silence that had gone out to the fields, were now to the roads, to the distance, to the West. That man whose mind had been bound with acres lived with narrow concrete miles. And his thought and his worry were not any more with rainfall, with wind and dust, with the thrust of the crops. Eyes watched the tires, ears listened to the clattering motors, and minds struggled with oil, with petrol, with the thinning rubber between air and road. Then a broken gear was tragedy. The water in the evening was the yearning, and food over the fire. Then health to go on was the need and strength to go on, and spirit to go on. The wills thrust westward ahead of them, and fears that had once apprehended drought or flood now lingered with anything that might stop the westward crawling.

Close reading

To interpret the writer's meaning we need to see how the sentences are connected by ideas which are developed throughout the text. The sentences that follow, when put together, form a paragraph about the situation of the migrant workers. Read the first sentence and the following four questions which suggest ways in which the paragraph might continue. Try to predict how the writer develops his ideas, then read the next sentence and check your prediction. Continue with the following sentences and questions, confirming or modifying your predictions, to the end of the paragraph.

Read:
> The cars of the migrant people crawled out of the side roads on to the great cross-country highway, and they took the migrant way to the West.

Predict:
Example:
a What were they going West for?
b Why were they using the highway?
ⓒ When did they travel?
d How many were travelling?

Check:
Read:
> In the daylight they scuttled like bugs to the westward; and as the dark caught them, they clustered like bugs near to shelter and to water.

Predict:
a Why did they camp together?
b How did they set up camps?
c When did they move on?
d Which was the more important, water or shelter?

Check:
Read:

> And because they were lonely and perplexed, because they had all come from a place of sadness and worry and defeat, and because they were all going to a new mysterious place, they huddled together; they talked together; they shared their lives, their food, and the things they hoped for in the new country.

Predict:
a What did they hope for?
b Who decided to camp in a certain place?
c How did they know where to stop?
d What reasons did different families have for camping in particular places?

Check:
Read:

> Thus it might be that one family camped near a spring, and another camped for the spring and for company, and a third because two families had pioneered the place and found it good.

Predict:
a Where would the pioneers go next?
b How many migrants might stop at each camp?
c What happened when night came?
d Which family had most motivation to stop?

Check:

> And when the sun went down, perhaps twenty families and twenty cars were there.

Scanning

The following extracts came from a novel called *Make Room! Make Room!* set in America in 1999 when the population has risen to 344 million.
Quickly find the answers to these questions in extract 1.
1 What is Steve Kulozik's job?
2 Where is he?
3 Why is he there?
4 What is the date?

Extract 1

'Half an hour more and we'll be in a new century,' Steve Kulozik said, stamping his feet on the icy pavement. 'I heard some joker on TV yesterday trying to explain why the new century doesn't start until next year, but he must be a chunkhead.
5 Midnight, year two thousand, new century. That makes sense.

Look at that.' He pointed up at the projection TV screen on the old Times Building. The headlines, in letters ten feet high, chased each other across the screen.

COLD SNAP IN MIDWEST SCORES OF DEATHS REPORTED

10   'Scores,' Steve grunted. 'I bet they don't even keep score any more, they don't want to know how many die.'

FAMINE REPORTS FROM RUSSIA NOT TRUE SAYS GALYGIN
PRESIDENTIAL MESSAGE ON MORN OF NEW CENTURY
NAVY SUPERSONJET CRASH IN FRISCO BAY

15   Andy glanced up at the screen, then back at the milling crowd in Times Square. He was getting used to wearing the blue uniform again, though he still felt uneasy when he was around any other men from the detective squad. 'What are you doing here?' he asked Steve.

20   'Same as you, on loan to this precinct. They're still scream-ing for reserves, they think there's going to be a riot.'

'They're wrong, it's too cold and there's not that many people.'

'That's not the worry, it's the nut cults, they're saying it's

25   the millennium, Judgement Day or Doomsday or whatever the hell you call it. There's bunches of them all over town. They're going to be damn unhappy when the world doesn't come to an end at midnight, the way they think it will.'

'We'll be a lot unhappier if it does.'

Close reading

Read extract 1 again and then tick the following statements as true (T) or false (F).

	T	F
a Steve is not sure when the new year starts.		
b Many people have died because of the cold weather.		
c It is not known exactly how many deaths there have been.		
d Some people expect trouble as the year changes.		

Word use: synonyms

What do you think the words in the first column mean as used in the text? Choose words from the second column that are most similar in meaning. Look them up in a dictionary if you are not sure.

joker (l. 3)	comedian/magician/fortune-teller
milling (l. 15)	pushing/restless/nervous
precinct (l. 20)	street/district/town
nut cults (l.24)	religious sects/mad people/criminal groups

Prediction: the continuation of a story

1 Indicate with a tick the way you predict the story will continue. Give two reasons for your choice. Then read extract 2.

   a The crowd riots as the New Year begins. □

   b The crowd celebrates the New Year peacefully. □

Extract 2

23:58—11:58 PM—ONE MINUTE TO MIDNIGHT

As the words slipped from the screen and were replaced by a giant clockface the crowd cheered and shouted; more horns sounded. Steve worked his way through the mass of people that filled the Square and pressed against the boarded-up windows on all sides. The light from the TV screen washed their blank faces and gaping mouths with flickering green illumination, as though they were sunk deep in the sea.

  Above them, the second hand ticked off the last seconds of the last minute of the year. Of the end of the century.

Did you predict correctly?

2 a–e are the beginnings of paragraphs which occur later in the story. Which one do you think follows immediately the above extract? Put the others in the order in which you think they occur in the story.

   a   Very faintly, Andy could hear the shrill of a police whistle from the direction of Forty-second Street. He worked his way toward the sound.

   b   'HAPPY NEW YEAR!' the thousands of massed voices shouted, 'HAPPY NEW CENTURY!' Horns, bells and noise-makers joined in the din.

   c   On the screen the President's face flicked out of existence with an almost-heard burst of music, and the flying, silent letters once more took its place.

   d   'End of the world!' a man shrieked, loud enough to be heard above the crowd, his spittle flying against the side of Andy's face. 'End of the world!'

   e   Above them the second hand had finished a complete circle, the new century was already one minute old.

Give reasons for your choice.

Anticipation

How do you expect the story to continue after the last extract? Tick the boxes according to your predictions.
L=Likely   P=Possible   U=Unlikely

a   Andy will become involved in some kind of trouble.
b   The crowds will start to go home.
c   Andy will meet someone he knows.
d   Andy will be killed.
e   Life will go on much as usual.
f   None of these things.

Check your predictions as you read extract 3.

Extract 3

Now, with their enthusiasm gone, the people were feeling the cold and the crowd was rapidly breaking up. Wide gaps appeared in their ranks as they moved away, heads bent into the icy wind from the sea. Around the corner on Forty-fourth Street, Hotel Astor guards had cleared a space so the pedi-cabs could come in from Eighth Avenue and line up in the taxi rank at the side entrance. Bright lights on the marquee lit up the scene clearly and Andy passed by the corner as the first guests came out. Fur coats and evening dresses, black tuxedo trousers below dark coats with astrakhan collars. Must be a big party going on in there. More bodyguards and guests emerged and waited on the sidewalk. There was the quick sound of women laughing and many shouts of 'Happy New Year!'

Andy moved to head off a knot of people from the Square who were starting down Forty-fourth Street, and when he turned back he saw that Shirl had come out and stood, waiting for a cab, talking to someone.

Suggest an ending for the story.

Evaluation of the text

There are many verbs of sound and movement in the extracts: list all those you can find. For example:

verbs of sound: grunted, . . .
verbs of movement: slipped, . . .

Why do you think the writer uses them? What effect do they create? Do you think the writer had any other reason for writing *Make Room! Make Room!* beyond telling a story of policemen in New York? What do you think is the significance of the title? Why do you think the writer set the story in the future?

Unit 3 **Travel**

Inference

Unfamiliar words

One of the major causes of worry for foreign language readers is what to do about unfamiliar words. The automatic reaction – to reach for a dictionary – is not only time-consuming and eventually demotivating, but also often unnecessary. (There is certainly a time and place for using a dictionary, but judiciously.) It is frequently possible to deduce the meaning of an unfamiliar word from a variety of clues – its place and function in the sentence, a possible similarity to words in other languages and, above all, its context. Deducing the meaning of unfamiliar words using these clues is one kind of inference.

Implied meaning

At a deeper level, every writer requires the reader to be able to deduce meaning which is not explicitly stated. The writer expects the reader to get from the text a certain amount of information which is not spelt out but which at the same time should be quite clear. This is popularly called 'reading between the lines' – it means understanding that which is only implied. This is another kind of inference, but operating on a larger scale than that of the individual unfamiliar word.

We are going to practise both types of inference in this unit. First we need to approach the text at the surface level (through anticipation, skimming, prediction and scanning) before we look at it in closer detail.

Section A

Anticipation

You are going to read an extract on travel in the Middle Ages. Before you read it, consider the statements below and tick each one T (true), F (false) or DK (don't know).

	T	F	DK
a Few people travelled in the Middle Ages.			
b Travel in the Middle Ages was dangerous.			
c Relatively more people travel today than in the Middle Ages.			
d People today travel in greater style than in the Middle Ages.			

Skimming for text-type

Look quickly at the extract on pages 38–9 and decide where it comes from. Tick one of the boxes below.
a ☐ a travel brochure
b ☐ a newspaper
c ☐ a book
d ☐ a magazine

Prediction

Which of the following would you expect to find in the extract? Before you skim for content, complete the first part of the table (I EXPECT).

	I EXPECT		I FOUND	
	YES	NO	YES	NO
a A discussion of the reasons why people travel.				
b An example of travel in the Middle Ages.				
c An example of contemporary travel.				
d A comparison between medieval and contemporary travel.				

Now skim the extract to see if your expectations are confirmed. Complete the second part of the table (I FOUND).

Scanning

Find the answers to these questions in the extract as quickly as possible.
1 Who was Thomas Becket?
2 Where was he going?
3 How many people was he travelling with?

Harried modern tourists, shuffling through crowded airports hung round with flight bags and cameras, are inclined to feel that no previous generation ever travelled so widely or responded so enthusiastically to the lure of distant places. They are certainly
5 convinced that no one in the remote Middle Ages ever went far from home or indulged themselves in foreign travel. The reality is quite different from this outdated stereotype, for even contemporary travel of the most luxurious kind would find it hard to compete with the elegance of the embassy of Thomas Becket to France in 1188.
10 William Fitzstephen, one of Becket's biographers, details with enthusiasm the elaborate spectacle that the travels of an important member of the medieval establishment could provide.
    On this occasion Becket's retinue as chancellor of England was made up of some two hundred members of his household – knights, clerks,
15 officials and young nobles sent to him for training. All were on horseback and dressed in new clothes suitable to their station in society. There were large iron-bound chariots, each pulled by five horses, and each having its own driver, guardian and fierce watch-dog. A groom walked beside each of the strong and shapely horses –
20 more like chargers, Fitzstephen says proudly, than your usual rather brokendown cart animals. Several of the chariots were earmarked for specific uses. One was set aside for transporting the requirements of the chapel, another for the chamber, one for the chancellor's exchequer and another for his kitchen. Two were required to transport
25 iron-bound barrels of fine English ale, 'that most healthy drink the colour of wine but of better flavour', which was intended as a gift for the French. The remaining carts carried food and drink for the company, bags of bedclothes, other bags of tapestries and hangings to decorate Becket's bed and chamber when he received guests, as well as the
30 miscellaneous baggage so truthfully described as impedimenta. At the

head of the twelve packhorses was the one carrying the altar ornaments,
sacred vessels and service books for the chancellor's chapel. The
others were loaded with chests of gold and silver vessels as well as
the more utilitarian plates and dishes, kettles and cauldrons. Other
35 chests carried Becket's supply of money (in pennies as the only actual
coins), sufficient for his daily expenses and all the expected gifts.
Among the remaining baggage were books and clothes, and the clothes at
least must have taken considerable space for the chancellor was
reported to have twenty-four complete changes with him, as well as
40 the elegant robes destined to be given away and left overseas. The
logistics of such a group would appal the most experienced modern
travel agent.

Close reading

Read the text carefully and decide if these sentences are true or false.

a The members of Becket's household wore a special uniform.
b The horses pulling the chariots were unusually fine animals.
c The food and drink for the company was carried by the packhorses.
d Becket took twenty-four sets of clothes for himself.
e Becket took drink and clothes as presents for the French.

Inference: unfamiliar words

You can see that you do not need to know the meaning of every word to be able
to get the main idea of a text, or to be able to answer some detailed questions.
Now we are going to look at how to work out the meaning of those unfamiliar
words you *do* want to understand.

There are four stages to this process:

1 Decide from your knowledge of English sentence structure and word-
   formation what part of speech (e.g. noun, adjective, verb or participle) the
   unfamiliar word is. Look at:
   a the unfamiliar word in relation to the words before and after it, e.g. 'the
      miscellaneous baggage' (l. 30). Because 'miscellaneous' follows the definite
      article and precedes a noun it must be an adjective.
   b the grammatical ending (—ed, —ing, —s, etc.), e.g. *shuffling* (l. 1). The
      ending —ing indicates a present participle or gerund.
   c the affix (a syllable attached to the beginning or end of a word, e.g. —er,
      —ment, —ous). This indicates meaning and sometimes tells you what part
      of speech the word is too, e.g. *establishment* (l. 12). The affix —ment indi-
      cates a noun.
2 Does the same word, or something similar, exist in your language? (English
   has taken words from Latin, French, German, Arabic and Hindi among
   others.) These similar-looking words are called *cognates*. But be careful –
   although they may look the same, they do not always have the same meaning.
3 Look at the context – what comes before and after the unfamiliar word – to
   decide on a meaning. You may find clues to the meaning in a previous, or
   later, sentence. Look around – and don't expect always to get the meaning
   absolutely clear the first time. It is usually enough for comprehension purposes to get the approximate meaning.

4 If stages 1–3 do not help you, and the unfamiliar word is blocking your comprehension of the text, use a dictionary. Using what you have worked out about the word in stages 1–3, fit the appropriate dictionary meaning into the context.

Look at the list of unfamiliar words below and the clues on page 41.
In column 1 mark what part of speech the word is.

Word	1	2	3
harried (l. 1)			
shuffling (l. 1)	participle		i verb of movement ii with difficulty
indulged (l. 6)			
establishment (l. 12)			
retinue (l. 13)			
charger (l. 20)			
earmarked (l. 21)			
chapel (l. 23)			
ale (l. 25)			
miscellaneous (l. 30)			
impedimenta (l. 30)			
altar (l. 31)			
utilitarian (l. 34)			
cauldrons (l. 34)			
appal (l. 41)			

In column 2 put a tick if you have a similar-looking word in your language.
In column 3 write down any ideas about the meaning that the clue on the facing page may give you.
Finally, check in a good English–English dictionary to see how close your inferences come to the dictionary definition.

One example – *shuffling* (l. 1) – has been done for you.

Clues

This adds to the picture of modern tourists. Look at the meaning of *shuffling* (l. 1). *Harried* is likely to have a similar negative connotation.

---

i What does the word *through* tell us about the participle *shuffling*?
ii *hung round with* shows that the tourists are carrying heavy, uncomfortable things. What kind of movement are they likely to be performing?

What opinion do you have of travel in the Middle Ages?
Do you imagine it was an everyday or exceptional activity?

You are a member of it – so what is it? A group? A club?

Who or what did the *retinue* consist of? What were they all doing with Becket?

Chargers are not like. . . but they are similar to. . . So a *charger* is a type of. . .

Look for the meaning in the next sentence. Can you explain the metaphor?

Look for the second time the word is used. Does this give you any help? What are *sacred vessels* and *service books*?

This is explained immediately. List five facts about *ale*.

What examples of baggage have *not* been mentioned so far?

The meaning is given, but can you explain the play on words?

Where would you find an *altar*? What would you put on it?

This word contrasts with two other adjectives in the sentence. What are they?

This appears as part of a list. What general word would include all the other things mentioned? What adjective describes *cauldrons*?

If a travel agent today was asked to organize such an expedition, how do you think he would feel?

Section B

Skimming for content

1 Look quickly over the text and decide if it is:
   a ☐ about a jungle
      ☐ about an underground railway
   b ☐ fact
      ☐ fiction
2 Look quickly over the text to decide if each of these sentences is true or false.
   a The writer describes travelling around the subway with two policemen.
   b The writer wants to show that the subway is not very safe.

The Underground Jungle

We were at Flushing Avenue, on the GG line, talking about rules for riding the subway. You need rules: the subway is like a complex – and diseased – circulatory system. Some people liken it to a sewer and others hunch their shoulders and
5 mutter about being in the bowels of the earth. It is full of suspicious-looking people.

I said, 'Keep away from isolated cars, I suppose.'
And my friend, a police officer, said, 'Never display jewellery.'
Just then, a man walked by, and he had Chinese coins – the old
10 ones with a hole through the middle – woven somehow into his hair. There were enough coins in that man's hair for a swell night out in old Shanghai, but robbing him would have involved scalping him.

***

'And don't sit next to the door,' the second police officer said. We were still talking about rules. 'A lot of these snatchers like to play the
15 doors.'

The first officer said, 'It's a good idea to keep near the conductor. He's got a telephone. So does the man in the token booth. At night, stick around the token booth until the train comes in.'

***

'Stay with the crowds. Keep away from quiet stairways. The
20 stairways at 41st and 43rd are usually quiet, but 42nd is always busy – that's the one to use.'

The man who said this was six-feet four, and weighed about twenty stone. He carried a ·38 in a shoulder holster and wore a bullet-proof vest. He had a radio, a can of Mace and a blackjack. He was a
25 plain-clothes man.

The funny thing is that, one day, a boy – five-feet six, and about ten stone – tried to mug him. The boy slapped him across the face while the plain-clothes man was seated on a train. The boy said, 'Give me your money,' and then threatened the man in a vulgar way. The
30 boy still punched at the man when the man stood up; he still said, 'Give me all your money!'

The plain-clothes man then took out his badge and his pistol and said, 'I'm a police officer and you're under arrest.'

'I was just kidding!' the boy said, but it was too late.

35 I laughed at the thought of someone trying to mug this well-armed giant.

'Rule one for the subway,' he said. 'Want to know what it is? Rule one is – don't ride the subway if you don't have to.'

***

Looking at Howard Haag and Joseph Minucci standing
40 on the platform at Nassau Avenue on the GG line, you would probably take them for a pair of physical-education teachers on the way to the school gym. They look tough, but not aggressively so; they are healthy and well-built – but some of that is padding: they both wear bullet-proof vests. Underneath the ordinary clothes the men are
45 well armed. Each man carries a ·38, a blackjack and a can of Mace. Minucci has a two-way radio.

***

'Look at that old lady,' Minucci said. 'She's doing everything wrong.'

The woman, in her late sixties, was sitting next to the door. Her
50 wristwatch was exposed and her handbag dangled from the arm closest to the door.

I wondered whether the plain-clothes men would warn her. They didn't. But they watched her closely, and when she got off they escorted her in an anonymous way. The old woman never knew how
55 well protected she was and how any person making a move to rob her would have been hammered flat to the platform by the combined weight of Officers Minucci and Haag.

Inference: unfamiliar words

Find the word(s) in the text that means:

a cutting the skin and hair off someone's head ....
b a police officer at work but not in uniform ....
c to rob with violence ....
d to hit with one's hand (two words are used –   i ....
    check their difference in meaning in a dictionary)   ii ....

Inference: implied meaning

Answer the following questions. Give reasons for your answers, based on the information in the text.

1 a How do you know the events described take place in an American city?
   b Why do you 'need rules' (l. 2) for riding the subway?
   c Why do people liken the subway to a 'sewer' (l. 4)?
   d What are 41st, 42nd, and 43rd?
   e How dangerous does the subway seem to be?
   f Why was the old lady 'doing everything wrong'? (l. 47–8)

g Why didn't the police warn her?
h How many 'rules for riding the subway' are mentioned? What are the reasons for each of them?

2 Note that there may be more than one answer to the following questions. Tick as many answers as you think correct.

i The writer mentions the story of the plain-clothes officer and the boy to show that on the subway
   a ☐ people can behave strangely.
   b ☐ people can play jokes on other travellers.
   c ☐ even children can be dangerous.
   d ☐ no one is safe.
ii The writer uses the story of the old lady as an example of
   a ☐ how no one recognizes the plain-clothes men.
   b ☐ how old people are more at risk.
   c ☐ how victims of crime can invite it.
   d ☐ how good the plain-clothes men are at their job.

Word use: synonyms

Can you give the British alternatives for the American words used here?

riding (l. 2) subway (l. 2) car (l. 7) swell (l. 13) conductor (l. 16)

Use a dictionary to check your ideas.

Evaluation of the text

1 Look at the title of the text. Which aspects of the jungle do you think the subway reflects? Choose the three adjectives you think describe it best and number them according to their relative effectiveness (1, 2 and 3). Give reasons for your choices.

   ☐ alien   ☐ dangerous   ☐ lawless
   ☐ complex   ☐ dark   ☐ wild
   ☐ damp   ☐ frightening

2 Which of the two experiences of travel considered in this unit seems to you the more dangerous? Give reasons for your choice.

   Have you ever travelled on the New York subway? If so, was it as dangerous as indicated in the text? If not, have you ever undertaken a dangerous journey?

Unit 4 **Language**

Cohesion

Sentences in texts do not stand in isolation but operate together with what has gone before and what comes after. We are now going to look at some of the ways in which sentences look backwards and forwards, and how the writer joins all the sentences together to make one coherent text.

Reference

The first area is that of *reference*, that is, the use of common words like 'he', 'she', 'it', 'this', 'that', 'one', 'so', etc. to refer to people, things or items of information already mentioned in the text. It is neither necessary nor considered good style to repeat information needlessly: the writer will not repeat a name where 'he' or 'she' will do. But obviously, to find the meaning of that word it is necessary to look outside the sentence, or the part of the sentence, in which it occurs, so use of context becomes crucial at this stage. As well as helping the writer avoid repetition, the use of reference helps tie the text together.

Ellipsis

Another area is *ellipsis*, the omission by the writer of information that can easily be provided by the surrounding text. For example, in 'He likes tea and she coffee' neither the writer nor the reader would feel it necessary for the word 'likes' to be repeated. In 'I told you not to', what it was I told you not to do can be clearly supplied from the context.

Discourse markers

The third area to consider is that of *discourse markers*. These are easily recognized 'signposts' which indicate how the writer has organized his text and reveals his intentions. For example, 'the second fact is that' shows that the writer is introducing a second point in his discourse.

Section A

Anticipation

1   How many verbs can you think of in English that could replace 'talk' (e.g., chat, discuss, gossip, etc.)? Make a list.

2   Organize your list into three columns:
    i   words generally used to describe only women talking
    ii words generally used to describe only men talking
    iii words which could be used for both sexes

3   What conclusions can be reached from considering these lists?

Skimming for function, text-type and content

Look quickly at the text on pages 47 and 48 and decide:

i what it is
   a ☐ an interview
   b ☐ a book review
   c ☐ a newspaper report
   d ☐ a personal column

ii where it appeared
   a ☐ a popular paper
   b ☐ a quality paper
   c ☐ a feminist paper
   d ☐ an academic journal

iii what it is about
   a ☐ men and language
   b ☐ women and language
   c ☐ men, women and language
   d ☐ contemporary language

Prediction

Which of the following would you expect to find in the text? Complete the first part of the table (I EXPECT).

	I EXPECT		I FOUND
a Examples of how men and women are served by language.			
b Examples of how men dominate language.			
c Scientific evidence that men dominate language.			
d No evidence, just anti-male propaganda.			
e Suggestions for improving the female position.			

Is there anything else which you would expect, or like, to find? If so, make a note of it before you read.

Close reading

Read the text on pages 47 and 48 carefully. When you have finished, complete the second part of the table (I FOUND). Were your expectations fulfilled or not? Are you satisfied with what you found? Would you have liked to find more on any of the points a–e?

Inference: unfamiliar words

Work out the meanings of the following words by considering word-formation, derivation and context.

irrefutable (l. 6)
hogging (l. 15)
termagant (l. 21)
enshrine (l. 32)
hassle (l. 58)

Word use: lexical sets

How many words can you find in the text that
i are connected with the verb 'talk'?
ii express male and female titles?
Make two lists.

Analyse the meanings of the listed words as they are used in the text by making
charts in the following way:

i

	M	F	Ø	–
talk	✓	✓	✓	
chatter		✓		✓

ii

	M	F	+	–
king	✓		✓	
queen	✓	✓	✓	✓

Key: M = male   F = female   Ø = neutral   + = positive   – = negative

Use a dictionary to help you.

Cohesion: reference

Look at the boxed words in the text on pages 47– 48. Draw lines from them to
the words, phrases or sentences that they refer to. The first two have been done
for you as examples.

Chatter   natter   prattle   nag   whine . . .

Dale Spender has a theory that the spoken word is heavily spiked with male chauvinism.
Sally Adams reports.

Men interrupt women more than women interrupt men. Men talk more than women.
These simple theories go against received/perceived wisdom but they are easy to demon-
5   strate in any mixed group.
   Test them out at your next dinner party. Staff meetings or work conferences are not
recommended for beginners; social occasions are safer.
   Dale Spender believes the male muscle in linguistics is irrefutable and has hundreds
of tape recordings to prove it. Her research has convinced her that a whole new approach
10   to language study is needed and this has not endeared her to male academic colleagues.
   She's tenacious, persistent and annoying. One man said, 'You make a problem every
time we talk.'
   'Now you know what it's like,' she replied.
   The problem is not solved by exposing it. For her it's a continuing struggle to get in
15   her 50 per cent's worth. Even when she thinks she's been hogging the conversation,
scrutiny afterwards shows she spoke only around 30 per cent.
   She won't be manipulated. 'They can't use "bitch" to pull me into line as they could
have done when I was 25.' She's 37. 'Instead of pushing me back into my place, it serves
as a reinforcement. When someone says, "You're a bitch" I know I'm doing the right
20   thing.'
   Sounds like a termagant? A front-line stormtrooper in the monstrous regiment? She's
a feminist but calls herself a 'closet heterosexual'. She's been living with the same fellow
for six years.

'Most of my friends haven't met him. I've no wish to make him an honorary woman.'
25 Every morning she cooks his breakfast. 'It's my vulnerability . . . But I do it because
it's not expected of me.' Men who live with feminists are very special, she says.

She's an Australian, with plenty of degrees and diplomas, who teaches women's
studies at the Institute of Education, University of London, edits *Women's Studies
International Quarterly*, and writes. She's currently working on *Women of Ideas*, a book
30 about the buried generations of women thinkers. *Man Made Language* is published on
Thursday. Men, she says, have encoded words and these contain an inherent bias to
silence women and enshrine male supremacy.

She's a passionate egalitarian, appalled by statistics like: women do four-fifths of the
world's work, earn one-tenth of the world's salaries, and own 1 per cent of the world's
35 wealth.

How does this relate to language? To her it's all about power. Consider male and
female titles and how the female ones have been downgraded. King OK, queen now
has added homosexual meanings; sir OK, dame has pantomime links; master OK,
mistress overt sexual meanings; courtier OK, courtesan now only sexual meanings.

40 Why is there no word for man talk equivalent to chatter, natter, prattle, nag, bitch,
whine and gossip? Why is there no four-letter shock word for rape as there is for
sexual intercourse? Rape is a respectable safe word, perfectly acceptable in polite
conversation. There's no taboo word to express the force, the trauma of rape. Why?
Could it be because the victim's experience is outside male awareness?

45 Dale says because men encoded the language, it is deficient for women's meanings.
There is no word, she says, which expresses being in the wrong just because you're a
woman. 'There's no word that sums up the fact that you start from a position of not
being an authority, not even on yourself.'

Sometimes old words are given new meanings. Spinning, for instance, used to
50 represent the journey feminists are making and is taken from spinster, evoking the whirling movement of creation.

Academics attack her, saying this is not linguistics, but that, she says emphatically
and triumphantly, is just her point. Linguistics is a male study of the language encoded
by men. They have this notion, she says, that they can say things more quickly and say
55 them better. But they are saying what words mean to them.

She started her research into language and sex 'by doing stupid things like counting
adjectives. Then I realized I had to look at people's assumptions.

'Why do they think women's language is deficient? Why was there a big hassle about
women announcers on the BBC? Who talks more? Who interrupts?'

60 Her credo is now clear. 'We need a language which constructs the reality of women's
autonomy, women's strength, women's power. With such a language we will not be a
muted group.'

Man Made Language, Dale Spender, Routledge & Kegan Paul.

Cohesion: ellipsis

Look at sentences i–iv and write them in full including any information that has
been omitted.
Example (l.7): social occasions are safer = social occasions are safer than work
occasions, such as staff meetings or work conferences.

  i (l. 13) 'Now you know what it's like,' she replied.
 ii (l. 15) ...her 50 per cent's worth.
iii (ll. 38–39) master OK, mistress overt sexual meanings;
 iv (l. 39) courtier OK, courtesan now only sexual meanings.

Summary

This is a summary of the content of the text but includes some mistakes. Correct these and rewrite the summary.

In this interview Dale Spender talks about his work researching the female dominance of language. He believes, but can't prove, that language was created by men, for men. For this reason he is popular with his male academic colleagues. But he admits that women talk much more than men. He asks why so many words that describe male character and activity should have negative meanings. Finally, he believes that language should be changed to reflect the experience of women more fairly.

Evaluation of the text

Do you agree with Dale Spender? If not, why not? If so, what should be done? How realistic are your suggestions?

Extraction of information

Write a short factual paragraph on Dale Spender for the jacket of her new book. Take the information from the text.

Section B

Anticipation

1 a How many languages or dialects do you speak at home with your family? If you speak more than one, say what and why.
   b How many languages are spoken in your country? If more than one, what is the national language and why?

2 Conduct a quick language survey of your class using the questions above. Record the results in the boxes below.
   a Number of people interviewed
   b Number of people who speak more than one language at home.
   c Number of people who speak a dialect at home.
   d Number of people who come from a country where more than one language is spoken.

Skimming for content

There are three paragraphs in the text on page 50. To which paragraph would you give the title:
a The Linguistic Consequences of the Marriage System
b The Geographical Distribution of the Languages

Scanning

Find the answers to these questions as quickly as you can.
1 Where is 'the area in question'?
2 How large is the area?
3 How many people live there?
4 What trade language do they speak?
5 What is the name for the natives' houses?

A real but exotic world

We . . .[1] turn to a real world, in which there is a great deal to be said about language in relation to society. It is the very exotic world of the north-west Amazon, described by A. P. Sorensen (1971) and J. Jackson (1974) (. . .[2] we shall see that things are not so very different in the kind of society to which
5   most of us are accustomed).

. . . ,[3] the area in question is half in Brazil and half in Colombia, coinciding more or less with the area in which a language called Tukano can be relied on as a lingua franca (i.e. a trade language widely spoken as a non-native language). It is a large area, . . .[4] sparsely inhabited; around 10,000
10   people in an area the size of England. Most of the people are indigenous Indians, divided into over twenty tribes, which are . . .[5] grouped into five 'phratries' (groups of related tribes). There are two crucial facts to be remembered about this community. . . .,[6] each tribe speaks a different language – sufficiently different to be mutually incomprehensible and, in some
15   cases, genetically unrelated (i.e. not descended from a common 'parent' language). ...[7] the *only* criterion by which tribes can be distinguished from each other is by their language. . . .[8] the five phratries (and ...[9] all twenty-odd tribes) are exogamous (i.e. a man must not marry a woman from the same phratry or tribe). . . . ,[10] it is easy to see the main linguistic consequences:
20   a man's wife *must* speak a different language from him.

. . . :[11] marriage is patrilocal (the husband and wife live where the husband was brought up), and there is a rule that the wife should . . .[12]
live where the husband was brought up... should use his language in speaking to their children (a custom that might be called 'patrilingual marriage').
25   The linguistic consequence of this rule is that a child's mother does not teach her own language to the child, . . .[13] a language which she speaks only as a foreigner – . . .[14] everyone in Britain learned their English from a foreign au-pair girl. One can . . .[15] hardly call the children's first language their 'mother-tongue' except by a stretch of the imagination. The reports of
30   this community do not mention any wide-spread disruption in language learning or general 'deterioration' of the languages concerned, . . .[16] we can assume that a language can be transmitted efficiently and accurately even under these apparently adverse circumstances, through the influence of the father, the rest of the father's relatives and the older children. . . . ,[17]
35   the wife goes to live in a 'long-house' in which the husband's brothers and parents also live, . . .[18] there is no shortage of contacts with native speakers of the father's language.

Word use: definitions

There are five specialist terms used in this text. Can you match each term to its correct definition?

exogamous   a husband and wife speaking the husband's language
lingua franca   b a grouping of tribes
patrilingual   c husband and wife living in the husband's birthplace
patrilocal   d language used between peoples whose native languages are
                     different
phratry   e marrying outside one's own group

Close reading

1 Consider the statements below and tick each one T (true) or F (false).

		T	F
a	People from two different tribes use a third language to communicate.		
b	A phratry is smaller than a tribe.		
c	More than twenty different languages are spoken in the area.		
d	No man in this area can marry outside his tribe.		
e	The wife must move to her husband's tribe.		
f	The child's first language is his father's.		

2 Choose the diagram which best represents the approximate composition of a typical long-house.

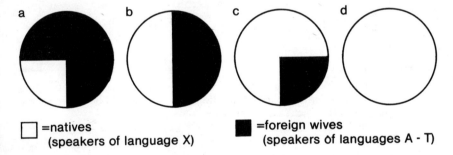

☐ =natives
   (speakers of language X)

■ =foreign wives
   (speakers of languages A - T)

Cohesion: discourse markers

This exercise looks at how the writer organizes his text and reveals his intentions. The words and phrases that act as 'signposts' (discourse markers) have been taken out and arranged under two broad headings, *Organization* and *Intentions*.

Organization
These signposts are used in this text to:

	Discourse markers
order and introduce the main points	first; geographically; now; the second fact is that; it is perhaps worth pointing out that; we now add a third fact
introduce an example	as though
subdivide a classification	in turn
draw a conclusion	putting these two facts together

Intentions
These signposts are used in this text to:

	Discourse markers
express cause or result	so; so; thus; thus
add something which the writer thinks is contrary to what has gone before or to what the reader would expect	but; but rather; indeed; not only . . . but also; though

Put these eighteen discourse markers back into their proper places in the text on page 50 (. . .[1], . . .[2], etc.).

Evaluation of the text

This text is about a patriarchal society (a society which is ruled and dominated by men). Explain how the particular situation described would be different in a matriarchy (a society which is ruled and dominated by women).

Unit 5 **Advertising**

Text analysis 1

Discourse

Sentences do not exist in isolation; nor can the full meaning of a text be understood simply by adding together all the meanings of each individual sentence. The meaning of the whole text is much more than the sum of its parts. When reading it is necessary to be able to understand not only what each sentence means by itself, but more importantly what it means within the whole text; how it relates to and adds to the rest of the text; and also what intentions the writer means to express. We are now operating at the level of *discourse*, that is, the way meaning and message are organized within the whole text.

We are going to look at discourse on three related levels.
  i *sentence level*
    Here the task is to analyze the functional or communicative value of individual sentences within a text.
 ii *paragraph level*
    Here the task is to re-order sentences into paragraphs and paragraphs into a whole text.
iii *whole-text level*
    Here the task is to identify the main idea of each section of the text.

Section A

Skimming for content

1 Look at the picture, the caption and the end of the advertisement. What is being advertised?

2 Look quickly over the text for a general idea of the content. Discuss your ideas.

A broken eggshell standing on tree trunk legs with a man's face at one end.

The man is balancing a tray on top of his head. On the tray is a set of pink bagpipes.

5 What exactly is going on in this painting?

But even more fascinating, what exactly was going on inside the artist Hieronymous Bosch's mind.

Was he *mad*? Mentally disturbed? Or was he a
10 perfectly normal sort of chap who just liked to paint weird 'goings-on'? Just to be different, perhaps?

We'll never really know. He died nearly five hundred years ago at the then ripe old age of sixty-six.

15 He leaves a lot of questions unanswered. In particular, what do we mean by 'normal'?

'Normal' thinking, 'normal' behaviour, 'normal' living.

But more significantly, how can we tell if the
20 mind is working normally, or abnormally?

You'd probably think you'd found the answer if you saw a man standing at a bus stop dressed as a bumble-bee. But not if you knew he was going to a fancy dress party.

25 However, if instead of his usual shirt and tie, the man started to turn up at work every morning dressed as an insect, you might be right in thinking he needed help.

Let's consider Brian, now seven years old.

30 When he was three, Brian and his teddy bear were inseparable. They'd go everywhere, do everything together.

Most children go through a phase like this. But sooner or later they lose interest in the object
35 they get attached to, and it gets set aside.

At six, Brian's obsession with his teddy bear got to a stage where he would never let go of it. And because his hands were full, he couldn't eat, play, read or write.

40 Any attempt to take the teddy away from him resulted in fierce, often violent, tantrums. Furniture was ripped, windows smashed.

Understandably, Brian's parents asked for help. There are many ways to help someone over-
45 come an obsession.

Could you ha
this mar

In Brian's case, slowly and carefully a Registered Mental Nurse (RMN) worked out a programm to separate Brian from his teddy. She was part of a highly professional team including clinical psy
50 chologists, psychiatrists and social workers.

At first, the nurse persuaded Brian to par with his teddy for just a second or two. Then te

Scanning

1 What job is being advertised here?
2 How long does the training for this job take?
3 What examples of mental illness are given here?

e unravelled
mind?

seconds. Then half a minute. Then two minutes.

Because of Brian's tantrums, an immense calmness and understanding of his problem were needed to help him through this first stage. Gradually, the time was increased when Brian was without his toy. During their separation the nurse introduced other activities.

As time went on (an RMN never expects quick results), short periods became long periods. Brian put his teddy away while he ate or went for a walk. 60

Later he could spend a whole day without his companion and go to school alone. 65

Although it may sound simple enough, helping a child overcome an overwhelming obsession with a teddy bear takes enormous skill.

In the same way it takes a great deal of intelligence and imagination to help a grown man over- 70 come a repeated urge to do unnecessary things, like continually rearranging cups on a table.

Or to help him come to terms with depression or anxiety caused by his wife leaving him. Or to make him feel needed after he has been made 75 redundant.

Perhaps nursing the mentally ill isn't a job you'd normally think of yourself doing.

It's by no means a 'normal' job. Assessing someone on the brink of suicide, working out a 80 plan of nursing care, putting it into action couldn't be further from a nine-to-five routine.

Certainly 'mental hospitals' are not what most people imagine them to be. Few people know that over half the patients admitted to psychiatric hos- 85 pitals are home again within a month. Or that many patients need never go near a hospital at all.

Because for most people being in hospital is a long way from the life they normally live, some psychiatric nurses spend most of their time work- 90 ing in the community, rather than in wards.

In one way, however, nursing the mentally ill is as normal as any other professional job.

The training takes three years. With hospital and community experience, practical assessment 95 and tough written exams.

In the end, unravelling and piecing together a man's mind introduces you to qualities in yourself you might never normally have discovered.

For more information, write to the Chief 100 Nursing Officer, P.O. Box 702 (MI/76), London SW20 8SZ.

Nursing

Inference: unfamiliar words

What do these words mean? Work out their meaning from their context (text and illustration).

unravelled	(caption)	tantrums	(l. 41)
bagpipes	(l. 4)	overwhelming	(l. 67)
weird	(l. 11)	on the brink of	(l. 80)
bumble-bee	(l. 23)	wards	(l. 91)

Word use: varieties of meaning

  i The word 'normal(ly)' is used eleven times in this advertisement. Find and underline every example and discuss the meaning of each. Can you explain the use of inverted commas ('—')?

 ii 'mental hospitals' (l. 83) is also in inverted commas. Can you explain why?

iii What words or phrases are used here as antonyms of the term 'mentally normal'? Make a list and explain any differences in meaning.

Text analysis 1: discourse at sentence level

1   Find an example in the text of each of the following functions:

    a describing
    b reporting
    c generalizing
    d exemplifying
    e explaining
    f stating a cause
    g stating a result
    h stating a contrast
    i asking a rhetorical question
    j answering a rhetorical question
    k inviting the reader to do something
    l making a suggestion to the reader
    m instructing the reader to do something

2   Find the introduction. Where does it end? How do the individual sentences in the introduction function? Use the list in question 1 to help you.

What is the importance of the introduction to the organization of the whole text?

Style

Describe the language used in this advertisement. Tick in the boxes as many descriptions as you think apt. Give reasons for your choice(s).

☐ familiar	☐ impersonal	☐ literary
☐ formal	☐ informal	☐ polite

Extraction of information

What do we learn from the advertisement about the job of an RMN? Make a list of the qualities needed for this work. Then add any further information about the job which you can find.

Evaluation of the text

Do you think the information in the advertisement is accurate and complete or that it has been carefully selected for the purposes of the advertisement? Do you think the advertisement is successful in its aims?

Section B

Anticipation

Look at the advertisement below. What do you think it is advertising? Can you explain the point of the picture?

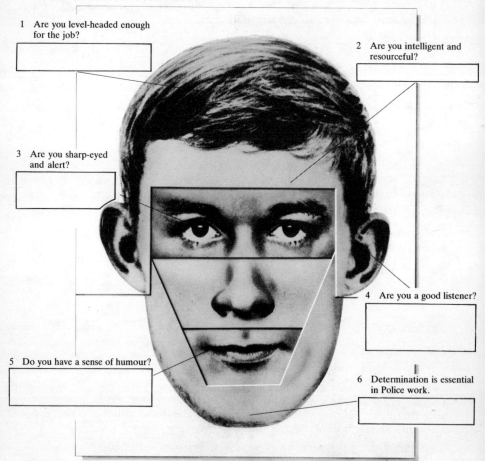

1 Are you level-headed enough for the job?

2 Are you intelligent and resourceful?

3 Are you sharp-eyed and alert?

4 Are you a good listener?

5 Do you have a sense of humour?

6 Determination is essential in Police work.

Are you wanted by the Police?

To: Police Careers (England and Wales). Dept. DE/0019, 6 Harrow Road, London W2 IXH. All vacancies are open to men and women. To join you must be a British subject, fit and at least 18½. Men must be at least 5'8" (172cms). Women 5'4" (162cms).
I am in full time education ☐   I am a Graduate ☐
Name (Mr/Mrs/Miss)
Address

Date of Birth

POLICE OFFICER

IF YOU'VE GOT A LOT TO OFFER US, WE'VE GOT A LOT TO OFFER YOU.

Close reading

This advertisement identifies six qualities (1–6) which it is considered are important for a potential police recruit to possess. a–f below describe six situations in
which these qualities would be necessary. Match the situations with the qualities,
e.g. 4 and a.

a
> At times you'll need to be
> sympathetic and tactful. Taking a
> statement, for example, from
> an elderly couple whose home has
> been ransacked.

b
> If you were to see a brawl on
> the street you'd have to step in
> and firmly control the situation.

c
> Someone's life could depend
> on your ability to think quickly.

d
> Lose your cool if you're abused
> by trouble-makers at a demo and
> you could have a riot on your hands.

e
> By noticing something
> suspicious about an
> apparently ordinary situation you may
> uncover a major crime.

f
> There are bound to be occasions
> when seeing the funny side of
> things will help you rise above the
> pressures of the job.

Inference: unfamiliar words

Work out the meanings of these words or phrases from their context and then
check your ideas in a dictionary.

ransacked   (box a)
brawl   (box b)
step in   (box b)
rise above   (box f)

Text analysis 1: discourse at paragraph level

Here is the text that accompanies the advertisement. There are eight short statements (a–h). Here they are given out of order. Can you put them in the correct
order? To help you do this, consider:
 i meaning
ii textual clues such as reference and discourse markers (see Unit 4)
Note that there may be differences of opinion about the order in which the
statements should appear. Be prepared to justify your choice.

a Starting with ten tough weeks at Police
   Training School, followed by two years
   on the beat.

c It's exactly the same for women as for
   men, and there are equal opportunities
   for promotion as well.

e Then, if you think you're the sort of
   person we want, send us an application
   form. The chances are we'll bring you in
   for questioning.

g Fill in the coupon and we'll send you our
   brochure.

b In London you'd be on £8,556 under 22,
   £10,290 over.

d But for those men and women who do
   have the personal qualities we are
   looking for in every Officer, there are
   prospects of a challenging and
   rewarding career.

f As you can imagine, not everyone who
   wants to join the Police is up to the
   demands of the job.

h You'd begin on £6,708 under 22, £8,442 if
   you're older.

59

Style

Describe the language used in this advertisement. Tick in the boxes as many descriptions as you think apt. Give reasons for your choice(s).

familiar ☐   impersonal ☐   literary ☐
formal ☐   informal ☐   polite ☐

Evaluation of the text

Can you explain these three informal expressions to do with the police?

wanted by the police
on the beat
bring you in for questioning

Two of them are used in the advertisement with different overtones from normal. Which are they? Can you explain the point of this? Do you think it is effective?

Section C

Anticipation

Consider these questions:

1 What are some of the functions of advertising?
2 Is there any commercial advertising in your country? If so, where and how can a person advertise?
3 Are there any things that cannot be advertised in your country? If so, what, and what are the reasons for this?
4 Is there any protection for consumers against offensive or misleading advertisements in your country?
5 Can you think of any advertisements that have offended you in any way?

Skimming for content

1 Look quickly at the heading and the end of the advertisement on page 61. What do you think it is about? In what way do you think the picture illustrates the message of the advertisement?

2 Read the introduction of the text down to '. . . and stopped' (l. 13). a–e below are the headings of the other five sections (1–5) of this advertisement. Read these first then skim each section and match it with its heading.
    a Why it's a two-way process
    b Whose interests do we really reflect?
    c What makes an advertisement misleading?
    d What do we do to advertisers who deceive the public?
    e How do we judge the ads we look into?

Scanning

Look quickly through the text and find the answers to these questions.

1 How many rules are there in The British Code of Advertising Practice?
2 Do these rules cover T V and radio advertising?
3 Why does the A S A encourage the general public to help it?

DO ADVERTISEMENTS SOMETIMES DISTORT THE TRUTH?

The short answer is yes, some do.

Every week many hundreds of thousands of advertisements appear for the first time.

5 Nearly all of them play fair with the people they are addressed to.

A handful do not. They misrepresent the products they are advertising.

10 As the Advertising Standards Authority it is our job to make sure these ads are identified, and stopped.

1

If a training course had
15 turned a 7 stone weakling into Mr Universe the fact could be advertised because it can be proved.

But a promise to build
20 'you' into a 15 stone he-man would have us flexing our muscles because the promise could not always be kept.

'Makes you look younger'
25 might be a reasonable claim for a cosmetic. But pledging to 'take years off your life' would be an overclaim akin to a promise of eternal youth.

30 A garden centre's claim that its seedlings would produce 'a riot of colour in just a few days' might be quite contrary to the reality.

35 Prose so flowery would deserve to be pulled out by the roots.

If a brochure advertised a hotel as being '5 minutes walk from the beach,' it must not require an Olympic athlete
40 to do it in the time.

As for estate agents, if the phrase 'over-looking the river' translated to
45 'backing onto a ditch,' there would be nothing for it but to show their ad the door.

2

Our yardstick is The British Code of Advertising Practice.

Its 500 rules give advertisers precise practical guidance on what they
50 can and cannot say. The rules are also a gauge for media owners to assess the acceptability of any advertising they are asked to publish.

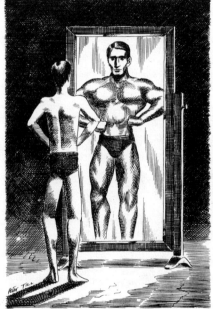

55 The Code covers magazines, newspapers, cinema commercials, brochures, leaflets, posters, circulars posted to you, and now commercials on video tapes.

The ASA is not responsible for TV and radio advertising. Though the

60 rules are very similar they are administered by the Independent Broadcasting Authority.

3

Unfortunately some advertisers are unaware of the Code, and breach
65 the rules unwittingly. Others forget, bend or deliberately ignore the rules.

That is why we keep a continuous check on advertising. But because of the sheer volume, we cannot monitor
70 every advertiser all the time.

So we encourage the public to help by telling us about any advertisements they think ought not to have appeared. Last year over 7,500 people
75 wrote to us.

4

Our first step is to ask advertisers

who we or the public challenge to back up their claims with solid evidence.

If they cannot, or refuse to, we ask them either to amend the ads or 80 withdraw them completely.

Nearly all agree without further argument.

In any case we inform the publishers, who will not 85 knowingly accept any ad which we have decided contravenes the Code.

If the advertiser refuses to withdraw the advertise- 90 ment he will find it hard if not impossible to have it published.

5

The ASA was not created by law and has no 95 legal powers.

Not unnaturally some people are sceptical about its effectiveness.

In fact the ASA was set 100 up by the advertising business to make sure the system of self control worked in the public interest.

For this to be credible, 105 the ASA has to be totally independent of the business.

Neither the chairman nor the majority of ASA council members is allowed 110 to have any involvement in advertising.

Though administrative costs are met by a levy on the business, no advertiser has any influence over ASA decisions. 115

Advertisers are aware it is as much in their own interests as it is in the public's that honesty should be seen to prevail.

If you would like to know more 120 about the ASA and the rules it seeks to enforce you can write to us at the address below for an abridged copy of the Code.

The Advertising ✓ 125
Standards Authority.
If an advertisement is wrong,
we're here to put it right.

ASA Ltd, Brook House,
Torrington Place, London WC1E 7HN. 130

4 How many people wrote to the ASA last year?
5 Does the ASA ask advertisers to remove immediately advertisements that have been challenged?
6 Who set up the ASA and why?
7 What is the ASA's slogan?

Inference: unfamiliar words

Work out the meanings of these words from their context and then check your ideas against the definitions and examples given in a dictionary.

play fair with	(l. 5)	circulars	(l. 56)	amend	(l. 80)
pledging	(l. 26)	breach	(l. 64)	contravenes	(l. 87)
akin to	(l. 28)	sheer	(l. 69)	sceptical	(l. 98)
seedlings	(l. 31)	monitor	(l. 69)	levy	(l. 114)
yardstick	(l. 46)	back up	(l. 77)	prevail	(l. 119)
gauge	(l. 51)				

Word use: antonyms

Find the word in the text with the opposite meaning to:

    weakling (look in section 1)
    knowingly (look in section 3)

Word use: word-play

1 Look at the five examples of misleading advertisements in section 1. In what way are they all misleading? List examples of this.

2 Explain these examples of word-play:
    a . . . would have us flexing our muscles . . . (l. 21–2)
    b Prose so flowery would deserve to be pulled out by the roots. (l. 35–6)
    c . . . but to show their ad the door. (l. 44–5)

Style

Describe the language used in this advertisement. Tick in the boxes as many descriptions as you think apt. Give reasons for your choice(s).

☐ familiar   ☐ impersonal   ☐ literary
☐ formal   ☐ informal   ☐ polite

Text analysis 1: discourse at whole-text level

Read the whole advertisement carefully. Summarize in one sentence only the main idea of each section. Then choose the best alternative (a–d) below.

    i *Introduction* (Do advertisements sometimes distort the truth?)
        a Advertisements often distort the truth.
        b A huge number of advertisements appear each week.
        c Most advertisements are quite truthful.
        d The ASA's job is to stop misleading advertisements.

ii *Section 2* (How do we judge the ads we look into?)
  a The ASA uses a detailed code to judge advertisements.
  b Advertisers can find practical guidance in The British Code of Advertising Practice.
  c Media owners can also consult The British Code of Advertising Practice.
  d The Code covers all types of media except TV and radio.

iii *Section 3* (Why it's a two-way process)
  a Some advertisers break the rules by accident.
  b The ASA has to keep a continuous check on advertising.
  c The ASA itself cannot monitor all the advertisements that appear.
  d The ASA relies on the general public to help it in its work.

iv *Section 4* (What do we do to advertisers who deceive the public?)
  a An advertiser has to produce solid evidence to support any claims made.
  b Most advertisers agree to amend or withdraw challenged advertisements.
  c If an ad is challenged the ASA informs both advertiser and publisher.
  d Publishers will not continue to accept challenged advertisements.

v *Section 5* (Whose interests do we really reflect?)
  a The ASA was set up by the advertising business itself and so has no legal powers.
  b It is in the interest of both the public and the advertising business that the ASA should operate effectively.
  c To maintain credibility the ASA has to be totally independent of the advertising business.
  d Although the advertising business pays for the ASA, no advertiser has any influence over ASA decisions.

Evaluation of the text

What is the point of this advertisement? Do you think it is successful in its aims?

Unit 6 **Psychology**

Text analysis 2

Within a text the writer expresses a central thought or a related group of ideas. There are a limited number of ways in which thoughts and ideas are expressed and this makes it possible to identify the thought patterns used in most texts. Of course, some writers structure their texts in unusual ways, but generally the textual organization is recognizable. In this unit two of the more common thought patterns will be considered in order to show how the writer organizes his ideas within a text.

Cause and effect

The particular relationship looked at is that between cause and effect (see Unit 5, *Text analysis 1: discourse at sentence level*). The work on reference in Unit 4 will prove useful in helping the reader to clarify argument. A text diagram on pages 66–7 shows the relationship between cause and effect within the structure of a text.

Contrast and comparison

The structure of the text and the way the writer contrasts and compares two pieces of information are considered here. Contrast and comparison are analyzed at paragraph level (see Unit 5, *Text analysis 1: discourse at paragraph level*).

Section A

Anticipation

Consider these questions:
1 How would you define *aggression*?
2 Where does aggression come from?
3 Is aggression always a destructive, negative force?
4 Can you draw a distinction between *aggression* and *aggressiveness*?

Skimming for content, text-type, function and tone

Skim the text and identify the content, text-type, function and tone.

One of the unfortunate features of the human condition is that the natural exploratory behaviour of human infants has to be curtailed, especially in conditions of civilization, where the hazards of traffic, electricity, gas, stairs and many other complex dangers have been added to those which are found in primitive, rural circumstances. We are forced to
5 overprotect our children psychologically, because we live in an artificial environment; and, because small children are ill-equipped to look after themselves when surrounded by the dangerous trappings of civilization, we tend to guard them too carefully in situations where this is not necessary.

In a recent experiment, Eleanor Gibson constructed a 'visual cliff'; that is, a floor which
10 appears to end in a sheer drop, but which is actually safe since the floor continues as a sheet of tough glass. Babies crawl to the apparent edge, but will not venture onto the glass even if encouraged to do so, since they are already aware of the danger of the drop. This is not to say that it is safe to leave a baby on the edge of a real cliff, since the child may turn round and fall off backwards.

15 The pioneer doctors who started the Peckham Health Centre discovered that quite tiny
children could be safely left in the sloping shallow end of a swimming bath. Provided no
adult interfered with them, they would teach themselves to swim, exploring the water
gradually and never venturing beyond the point at which they began to feel unsafe. Similarly, children would teach themselves to ride bicycles and use gymnasium equipment, and

20 did so more confidently and quickly than if adults tried either to urge them on or warn
them to be careful. The American analyst Clara Thompson writes:

> Aggression is not necessarily destructive at all. It springs from an innate tendency to
> grow and master life which seems to be characteristic of all living matter. Only when
> this life force is obstructed in its development do ingredients of anger, rage, or hate

25 > become connected with it.[1]

It is a pity that our culture makes such obstruction inevitable: and one reason why aggressiveness is a problem to modern man is that the natural exploratory urge to grasp and master
the environment has perforce to be limited in a way which is bound to cause frustration.
There are far too many things which children must not do or must not touch; so that within

30 all of us who have been brought up in Western civilization, especially in urban civilization,
there must be reserves of repressed, and therefore dangerous, aggression which originate
from the restrictions of early childhood.

[1]Thompson, Clara M., *Interpersonal Psycho-Analysis*, Basic Books, New York, 1964.

Close reading
Decide if these sentences are true or false.

a There are fewer and less complex dangers for infants in primitive rural
  cultures.
b The natural exploratory behaviour of infants is restricted in every society.
c Babies do not react to a drop in the floor or ground in front of them.
d Babies learn to swim better on their own.
e An essential part of aggression is anger.
f One of the causes of aggressiveness is frustration in early childhood.

Word use: equivalents
Find the word in the text with the equivalent meaning to:

characteristics	be bold enough to do something risky
limited	someone who does something first,
dangers	prepares the way for others
the extra parts, the accessories	inborn
a high, steep rock facing the sea	seize and hold
very steep, vertical	necessarily

Cohesion: reference and ellipsis
What do these words refer to?

a those (l. 4)   d them (l. 17)
b this (l. 8)   e did so (l. 20)
c to do so (l. 12)   f such (l. 26)

Text analysis 2: cause and effect

Below is a diagram which represents the relationship between cause and effect which is developed in the text. Complete the text diagram by:
1 filling in the boxes with the correct information taken from the text
2 filling in the lozenges with the correct discourse marker (because/as a result)

paragraph 1

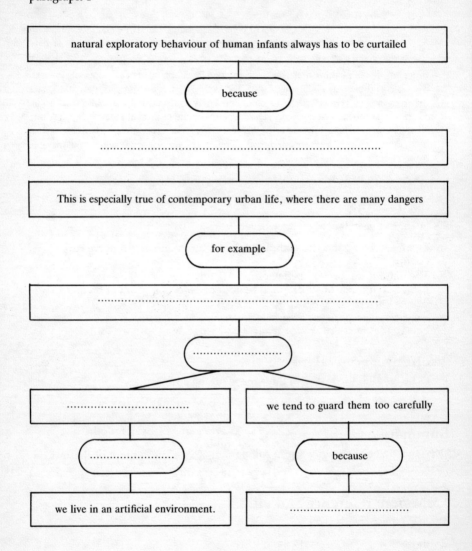

paragraphs 2 and 3

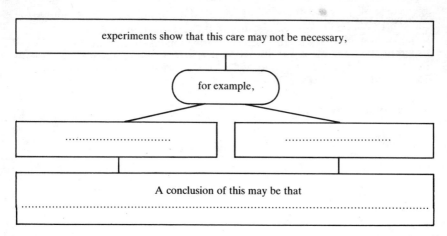

experiments show that this care may not be necessary,

for example,

....

A conclusion of this may be that

paragraph 4

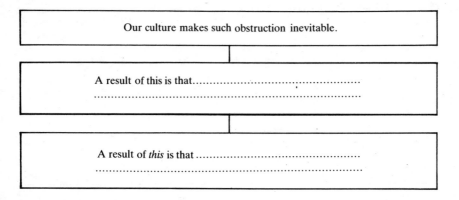

Our culture makes such obstruction inevitable.

A result of this is that...

A result of *this* is that ....

Summary

Use your notes above to write in full a summary of the content of the text on pages 64–5.

Evaluation of the text

Do you think frustrated aggression is a problem only for those of us 'who have been brought up in Western civilization' (l. 30)?

Section B

Anticipation

'The Pleasure Machine' is the title of an article describing recent psychological experiments. Before you read the first extract, write down as many pleasurable experiences as you can (e.g. the smell of freshly made coffee, reading a poem). Then try to guess what the Pleasure Machine is.

Skimming for content

Read quickly through extract 1 and discover what the Pleasure Machine is. Was your guess correct?

THE PLEASURE MACHINE

Extract 1

Psychological theorists once considered pleasure an important catalyst of human action. It was so influential that Freud elevated it to principle, arguing
5 that all human life is a struggle between life instinct, the attempt to get as much pleasure as possible, and death instinct, the wish to give it all up and return to dust.
10 Yet during the last two decades pleasure has suffered a period of neglect. It was too abstract a concept for experimenters. They could gauge the effects of tangible rewards, like offering
15 a research rat pellets of food... But pleasure itself remained difficult to define – one person's pleasure being another's pain – and it was almost impossible to quantify...
20 Today, however, pleasure seems to be making a comeback. Researchers Randy Thomas and Tim Brock, of Ohio State University, have developed a machine that measures pleasure. The
25 device is a variation of Stanley Milgram's famous pain seat. Instead of delivering the vicious electrical shocks that Milgram required for his study of obedience, however, the pleasure
30 machine treats sitters to exquisite, sensual vibrations.
   The subject sits on a pad placed in the seat of a comfortable chair. At the touch of a button, the pad produces
35 undulating nirvana. Subjects in Thomas and Brock's surveys rhapsodized about the intense pleasure of the feelings they received. In one test, subjects were allowed to give
40 themselves the experience of pressing the button that set the seat vibrating. Some hedonists, the researchers discovered, hogged more than 15 minutes of absolute personal pleasure.
45 Then the scientists had trouble persuading them to stand up and go home.
   But the question Thomas and Brock wished to address with their chair
50 wasn't self-satisfaction. They wanted to explore the patterns of pleasure giving between strangers. To this end, they adapted the format of Dr Stanley Milgram's classic experiment in
55 obedience. In that test Milgram asked subjects to deliver what appeared to be dangerous, and sometimes fatal, electrical shocks to strangers. He found that few refused.
60 The Ohio State team, by contrast, offered strangers the opportunity to give pleasure to one another. Thomas invited subjects to his lab, showed them the pleasure machine, and then
65 told them they would have the chance to deliver intense pleasure to someone just by pressing a button.

Scanning

Find the answers in extract 1 to these questions as quickly as possible.

1 Which psychologist thought pleasure was the main factor in human life?
2 For how long was the study of pleasure abandoned?
3 What was the name of Milgram's machine?
4 Who conducted tests in obedience?
5 What was the longest time spent on the pleasure machine?

Word use: synonyms

Look at the twelve words in the lefthand column below and try to guess their meaning from their function and context in the extract. Then, with the help of a dictionary if necessary:

a match each word in the lefthand column to the correct synonym (there are four each of verbs, nouns and adjectives)
b discuss the meanings of the pairs of words
c consider whether the synonyms could be used in the text in place of the unfamiliar words, and if not, why not?
d form new sentences showing the differences between the words in the lefthand column and their synonyms

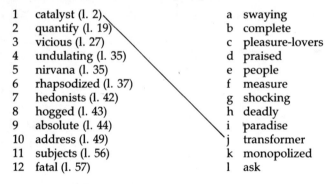

1	catalyst (l. 2)	a	swaying
2	quantify (l. 19)	b	complete
3	vicious (l. 27)	c	pleasure-lovers
4	undulating (l. 35)	d	praised
5	nirvana (l. 35)	e	people
6	rhapsodized (l. 37)	f	measure
7	hedonists (l. 42)	g	shocking
8	hogged (l. 43)	h	deadly
9	absolute (l. 44)	i	paradise
10	address (l. 49)	j	transformer
11	subjects (l. 56)	k	monopolized
12	fatal (l. 57)	l	ask

Text analysis 2: contrast

The writer organizes his thoughts in this extract mainly by the use of contrast. He signals his intention by the use of certain contrast markers such as 'however', 'yet', 'but', etc. The contrast pattern often contains one positive and one negative idea.

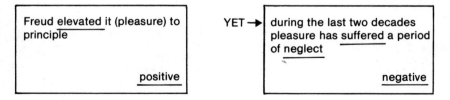

Freud elevated it (pleasure) to principle	YET →	during the last two decades pleasure has suffered a period of neglect
positive		negative

1 Find other examples of contrast in the extract.
2 Complete the diagram with ideas connected by contrast markers.
3 Identify the positive or negative ideas.

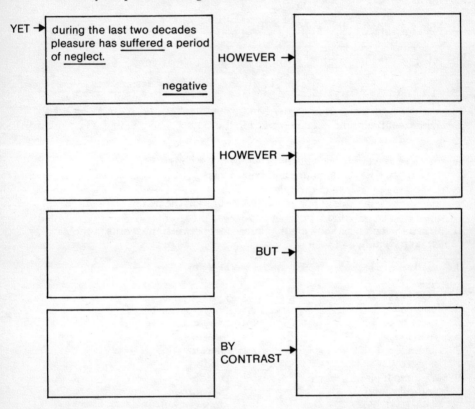

Summary

Taking your information from the diagram, write a summary of extract 1.

Section C

Prediction

Read the end of extract 1 again and decide how you expect the article to continue. Choose a, b, c or d.

a Some of the subjects refused to give each other pleasure.
b The majority of the subjects left the laboratory.
c A minority of the subjects wanted to give pleasure.
d A few of the subjects wanted to give pain not pleasure.

Close reading

1 Read the first paragraph of extract 2 on page 71 and see if you were correct in your prediction.

2   Now read the rest of extract 2 and decide if the following statements are true or false.

	T	F
a It was possible to receive a great deal of pleasure irrespective of one's social standing.		
b Men gave women more pleasure than women gave men.		
c Attractive people gained more pleasure than unattractive ones.		
d When engaged couples were tested the results had no validity.		
e People involved in close relationships preferred artificial pleasure.		
f By the year 2100 people will be interacting with machines.		
g People get more pleasure from each other than from pleasure machines.		

Extract 2

Thomas and Brock found, to their surprise, that far more people refused to give pleasure than refused Milgram's offer to give pain. Ten percent of the
5 subjects stalked out of the lab saying that the experiment was dirty, immoral, and beneath their dignity. Of those who did take part, Thomas reported, most enjoyed the experience. One man said,
10 "It's a unique way of getting to know people" by giving them a bucket full of pleasure.

The Ohio State study found that certain rules seem to apply to pleasure giving.
15 If, for instance, the person in the chair is perceived as being of high social status, he gets more pleasure than others would. Also, pleasure giving works better with heterosexual pairs.
20 Men gave women more intense and longer bouts of pleasure than they gave other men. And women were just as conventional. They preferred to press the button for men rather than for other
25 women. Thomas also asked subjects to rate how attractive the person in the pleasure chair appeared; he found that the more attractive the person, the more pleasure he or she received.
30 One doubt dogged the Ohio State experimenters. Could their research be invalidated if the subject and control gave each other pleasure before being tested? Dating couples, Thomas
35 reasoned, had the chance to give each other real pleasure, body to body, rather than artificial pleasure, button to button. So, he thought, dating couples might scoff at the machine. Not at all.
40 Dating couples spent more time giving each other pleasant vibrations than did all the other twosomes. Clearly, the more intimately people knew each other, the more reciprocal pleasure they were
45 willing to offer.

Some social scientists have predicted a future of impersonal sex in which the human race has abandoned carnal pleasures in exchange for being
50 seduced and caressed by all kinds of electronic wonder devices. The experiment in Ohio suggests, however, that part of the good derived from the pleasure machine is the joy of knowing
55 that another human being controls the buttons that deliver the right vibrations. Probably, even by A.D. 2100, Thomas concludes, the best pleasure won't come from machines but through interaction
60 between people.

Inference: implied meaning

Consider these questions, taking your ideas from the text.

1 Why should ten percent of the subjects feel the experiment was 'dirty, immoral, and beneath their dignity'?
2 For what reason was a person of high social status given more pleasure?
3 Why did dating couples give each other more pleasure than other twosomes?
4 Why should social scientists predict a future of impersonal sex?

Text analysis 2: comparison

Comparison in a text can be indicated by markers that point to similarities or differences, for example, 'more... than' or 'less... than'. Consider the sentence 'Far more people refused to give pleasure than refused to give pain.'

1 Find examples of comparison in extract 2 that relate to:

> social status   men   women   couples

Write out the sentences and indicate the markers.

2 Find two examples of contrast in extract 1, identify the markers and indicate the positive and negative ideas concerned.

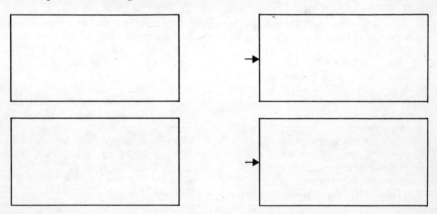

Evaluation of the text

Why do you think people are less willing to give pleasure than to inflict pain? Support your opinions with reference to the complete text.

Unit 7 **Art**

Visual comprehension

Visuals (pictures, diagrams, charts, etc.) are often used by the writer to assist the reader in the comprehension of a text. This is particularly true of descriptions and explanations of systems and processes. To understand what the writer is trying to communicate, the reader must be able to see the same visual, or to recognize the same information within the visual, as the writer.

Picture response

In the first part of this unit the reader has to respond to a visual (in this case a painting), as well as evaluate other people's responses to the same visual. The reader looks from the visual to the text and back again.

Text response

The second part of this unit is concerned with the visualization of information presented in the text. The process is reversed: the reader looks *from* a text *to* a visual and back again, using the text to create a visual.

Section A

Anticipation

This text is divided into seven sections.
Look at section 1 on page 74.
1 Describe as precisely as possible what you can see.
2 Describe the expressions on the faces of the man and woman. What sort of character do you think each of them had? Would you like to meet either of them today at a party?
3 What impression do you think the man's clothes are intended to convey? And those of the woman?
4 Why do you think this couple is painted in front of this particular background?
5 The title of this painting is simply *Mr and Mrs Andrews*. Can you suggest another title which would make your interpretation of the picture more explicit?

Skimming for function and text-type

Look quickly over the whole text and decide:

i whether it aims to
a ☐ tell a story
b ☐ present an argument
c ☐ solve a problem
d ☐ give a description

ii whether it comes from
a ☐ a museum catalogue
b ☐ a magazine article
c ☐ a political pamphlet
d ☐ a book on art

1   **Consider the well-known example of Gainsborough's** Mr and Mrs Andrews.

2   **Kenneth Clark* has written about Gainsborough and this canvas:**

5
At the very beginning of his career his pleasure in what he saw inspired him to put into his pictures backgrounds as sensitively observed as the corn-field in which are seated Mr and Mrs Andrews. This enchanting work is painted with such love and mastery that we should have expected

10
Gainsborough to go further in the same direction; but he gave up direct painting, and evolved the melodious style of picture-making by which he is best known. His recent biographers have thought that the business of portrait painting left him no time to make studies from nature . . .

15
His real opinions on the subject are contained in a letter to a patron who had been so simple as to ask him for a painting of his park: 'Mr Gainsborough presents his humble respects to Lord Hardwicke, and shall always think it an honour to be employed in anything for His Lordship; but with

20
regard to *real views* from Nature in this country, he has never seen any place that affords a subject equal to the poorest imitations of Gaspar or Claude.'

*Kenneth Clark, *Landscape into Art* (John Murray, London)

3   **Why did Lord Hardwicke want a picture of his park? Why**
25   **did Mr and Mrs Andrews commission a portrait of themselves with a recognizable landscape of their own land as background?**

4   **They are not a couple in Nature as Rousseau imagined nature. They are landowners and their proprietary attitude towards what surrounds them is visible in their stance and their expressions.**

5
30   **Professor Lawrence Gowing has protested indignantly
against the implication that Mr and Mrs Andrews were interested in
property:**

> Before John Berger manages to interpose himself again
> between us and the visible meaning of a good picture,
35   > may I point out that there is evidence to confirm that
> Gainsborough's Mr and Mrs Andrews were doing
> something more with their stretch of country than merely
> owning it. The explicit theme of a contemporary and
> precisely analogous design by Gainsborough's mentor
40   > Francis Hayman suggests that the people in such
> pictures were engaged in philosophic enjoyment of 'the great
> Principle . . . the genuine Light of uncorrupted and
> unperverted *Nature*.'

6
45   **The professor's argument is worth quoting because it is
so striking an illustration of the disingenuousness that bedevils the
subject of art history. Of course it is very possible that Mr and Mrs
Andrews were engaged in the philosophic enjoyment of unperverted Nature.
But this in no way precludes them from being at the same time proud
landowners. In most cases the possession of private land was the
50   precondition for such philosophic enjoyment – which was not uncommon
among the landed gentry. Their enjoyment of 'uncorrupted and
unperverted nature' did not, however, usually include the nature of other
men. The sentence of poaching at that time was deportation. If a man stole
a potato he risked a public whipping ordered by the magistrate who
55   would be a landowner. There were very strict property limits to what
was considered *natural*.**
7   **The point being made is that, among the pleasures their
portrait gave to Mr and Mrs Andrews, was the pleasure of seeing
themselves depicted as landowners and this pleasure was enhanced by
60   the ability of oil paint to render their land in all its substantiality. And
this is an observation which needs to be made, precisely because the
cultural history we are normally taught pretends that it is an unworthy
one.**

Scanning

Which of the three art historians (Clark, Gowing or Berger) used these phrases or sentences to express their opinions of the painting?

Scan the text, decide who the speaker is and put a tick in the correct column.

	Clark	Gowing	Berger
a . . . his pleasure in what he saw inspired him.			
b . . . backgrounds as sensitively observed . . .			
c This enchanting work . . .			
d . . . painted with such love and mastery . . .			
e . . . a recognizable landscape of their own land as background?			
f They are landowners . . .			
g . . . their proprietary attitude towards what surrounds them . . .			
h . . . Mr and Mrs Andrews were interested in property.			
i . . . the visible meaning of a good picture . . .			
j . . . Mr and Mrs Andrews were engaged in the philosophic enjoyment of unperverted Nature.			
k . . . proud landowners.			
l . . . the pleasure of seeing themselves depicted as landowners . . .			
m . . . the ability of oil paint to render their land in all its substantiality.			

Close reading

This extract can be divided into seven sections (1–7) according to the development of the argument. The function of each section within the argument is described below. Match each description with its section, and write each number in the correct box (a–g).

a   ☐ Berger dismisses Gowing's argument.
b   ☐ Berger quotes Clark's opinion of the painting.
c   ☐ Berger gives us his interpretation through direct reference to the painting.
d   ☐ Berger introduces the example of Mr and Mrs Andrews.
e   ☐ Berger quotes Gowing's rejection of his interpretation.
f   ☐ Berger restates his own interpretation of the painting.
g   ☐ Berger uses rhetorical questions to focus the reader's attention on his own interpretation of the painting.

Word use: dictionary use

What do these words mean? Use a dictionary to find out. First, remove the affixes from each word (see Unit 3, p. 39) to find the head word, e.g. dis-*ingenuous*-ness.

disingenuousness	(l. 45)
poaching	(l. 53)
whipping	(l. 54)
enhanced	(l. 59)

Inference: unfamiliar words

1 What do these words mean? Work out their meanings from word-formation, derivation and context.

proprietary	(l. 28)
stance	(l. 29)
bedevils	(l. 45)
precludes	(l. 48)
deportation	(l. 53)

2 What do these words mean in the context of this extract? Consider the range of possible meanings.

mastery	(l. 9)
direct	(l. 11)
melodious	(l. 11)
simple	(l. 16)
affords	(l. 21)
uncorrupted	(l. 42)
unperverted	(l. 43)
render	(l. 60)
substantiality	(l. 60)

Visual comprehension: picture response

1 Evaluate Gowing's attitude to Berger, and Berger's to Gowing. Look carefully at the *tone* of language used.

2 Gowing talks about the 'visible meaning of a good picture'. But we have seen three different interpretations of the same picture from three art historians. Which do you agree with, and why? Do you find support for your opinion within or outside the painting?

Section B

The Young Cicero Reading

Anticipation

1 Can you explain the different techniques used in:
an oil painting a watercolour a drawing a print a fresco?
2 What effect do you think the use of different materials and different techniques has on a work of art?
3 Compare the fresco above with the oil painting on p. 74.

Close reading

What materials are needed to paint a fresco? Read the text carefully and make a list.

Let us now describe the stages by which frescoes were executed. Since artists in the fourteenth and fifteenth centuries did not feel humiliated by the task of preparing personally every detail of their work, they themselves spread on the wall the *arriccio*, a rough layer of coarse plaster whose surface was uneven so that the upper
5 layer of plaster (or *intonaco*) could adhere to it. It was on this second layer that the painting was executed. A fine cord, soaked in red paint, fastened at each end and pulled taut, was pressed or 'beaten' against the wall, so that it left a mark on the *arriccio*. This established the centre of the space to be painted. When the space was large, the cord was used more than once to make a number of vertical and
10 horizontal divisions in it. The artist then drew in charcoal,[1] directly on to the *arriccio*, the design of the painting he was to make, correcting it if necessary until he was completely satisfied. With a small pointed brush dipped in a thin solution

of ochre[2] which left only a light imprint, he went over the charcoal drawing, which
was then erased with a bunch of feathers. The faint ochre was then retraced and
15 reinforced with *sinopia* red, and when this was done the preparatory drawing for
the painting was complete. These large mural drawings (which are now called
sinopie after the special red earth in which they were carried out) disappeared from
sight under the wet *intonaco*, and only come to light again when the paint surface
of a fresco is detached. No matter whether they are finished with great precision
20 or show traces of rapid, summary execution – this varies from artist to artist
according to the importance each attached to this preparatory work – *sinopie* are
always of the greatest interest, not only because they are often very beautiful (they
were always executed by the master himself, unlike the fresco where pupils and
assistants intervened) but also because they are almost the only drawings that
25 survive from early times, when it was not a common practice to draw on paper or
parchment.[3] *Sinopie* could also serve to give the donor who commissioned the work
a clear idea of how it would look when it was finished, and there are numerous
cases in which one can infer that the patron insisted on changes in the composition.
They were not, however, intended to be permanently visible or to be exposed to
30 public view. Consequently the *sinopia* constitutes the purest expression of the
artist's personality, one in which he is not compelled to follow the conventions of
his period. Because they are a free expression of the painter's consciousness, *sinopie*
sometimes seem altogether alien to the time in which they were produced. When
the *sinopia* was complete, the artist began his fresco by spreading the smooth
35 *intonaco* on the *arriccio*. In true fresco technique he applied only as much *intonaco*
as he could paint and finish between the morning and evening of one day. Although
the *sinopia* disappeared under the new plaster, the essential lines of the hidden
drawing were rapidly retraced on the *intonaco*. So the fresco came into being.

[1]A sort of thick pencil made from burnt wood.
[2]Yellow earth which was mixed with liquid to make a sort of paint.
[3]Good quality paper (originally it was made from animal skin).

Word use: definitions

Match these specialist terms used in the text to their definitions:

arriccio	a	the upper layer of fine plaster
intonaco	b	a large preparatory wall drawing
sinopia	c	the lower, rough layer of coarse plaster

Word use: antonyms

Find the words or phrases in the text which have the opposite meanings of those
listed below.

Example: fine   coarse (l. 4)

even	unfinished
lower	disappear
horizontal	slow-moving
blunt	detailed
strong	temporarily
	rough

Word use: equivalents

Find the more formal equivalent used in the text for the words listed below.

Example: job   task (l. 2)
stick (*verb*)   rubbed out
carried out   gone over
fixed   finished (*adjective*)
tight (*adverb*)   marks (*noun*)
straight (*adverb*)   a lot of
          forced

Close reading

Tick the following sentences as true (T) or false (F).

	T	F

a The artist did not spread the *arriccio*.
b The artists' pupils and assistants helped with the *sinopie*.
c Artists of the fourteenth and fifteenth centuries did not usually draw on paper.
d Changes were sometimes made between the *sinopia* and fresco.
e The *sinopia* was always covered by wet plaster.
f The fresco was painted directly on the *arriccio*.

Inference: implied meaning

Consider these questions. Take your ideas from the text.

1 What does the writer suggest when he says that 'artists in the fourteenth and fifteenth centuries did not feel humiliated by the task of preparing personally every detail of their work'?
2 Why were there two layers of plaster?
3 Why did the artist make horizontal and vertical divisions on the *arriccio*?
4 Why did the artist go over the charcoal drawing in ochre and *sinopia* red?
5 Why did the artist only spread the *intonaco* bit by bit?
6 How many preparatory stages were there to painting a fresco?
7 How valuable to art lovers and art historians is the new technique of removing the painted surface of a fresco?

Visual comprehension: text response

1 This drawing represents one of the eight stages involved in the painting of a fresco as described in the text. Look carefully at the text and match the drawing to the correct stage, giving the line reference.

2 Draw the next stage in the process yourself.

Unit 8 **Technology**

Visual classification

Diagrams and pictures will often help with, and sometimes be essential to, the interpretation of a text. They are frequently the quickest way to present complex information, which might otherwise take several pages of text to explain. This is particularly true when the text is concerned with technology or science.

Relationship between text and visuals

Section A of the unit shows how illustrations are used to support a text.
Section B of the unit shows how illustrations are integrated with a text to clarify instructions

Use of diagrams as classification

In Section C of the unit, diagrams show how information can be classified in an easily understood form. Diagrams can present a large amount of complicated information in a precisely classified form which is both quicker to examine and easier to understand than several paragraphs of scientific or technological writing.

Section A

Anticipation

You are going to read about the Persian Wheel, a traditional waterwheel, first used in the Middle East. Before reading the text, consider the statements below and mark each one T (true), L (likely), P (possible), U (unlikely) or F (false).

		T	L	P	U	F
a	The Persian Wheel is an expensive way to obtain water.					
b	Water is important in the Middle East.					
c	It is easy to make a Persian Wheel.					
d	The Persian Wheel is worked by animals.					
e	Craftsmen in the village make the wheel.					

Scanning

Find the answers to these questions in extract 1 as quickly as possible.

1 Which water-lifting device is the fastest?
2 Where are the buckets made?
3 What do the children look after?
4 Who understands how the wheel is constructed?
5 Is a pump or a waterwheel more appropriate for the village?

Extract 1

In some villages a different water-lifting device is used which lifts water faster
than the balancing trough, but not as fast as the diesel pump. It does not
require such hard work and can be made in the village. It's called a Persian Wheel.
The buckets lift the water from the stream and empty it into the channel. The
5   wheel itself is turned by a bullock that is looked after by some of the village children.
        The buckets are made by the village blacksmith out of tins and. If the Persian
Wheel breaks down the blacksmith understands how it's made and can repair it. This
is a technology that is better than the traditional one and is more appropriate to
the village than the diesel or electric pump.

A

B

Visual classification: illustrations to support a text

Look at pictures A and B, read extract 1 again carefully, and then decide which
picture is of the Persian Wheel. Explain your choice.

Inference: unfamiliar words

1 Work out the meanings of the following words from their context.

trough   (l. 2)
bucket   (l. 4)
stream   (l. 4
channel   (l. 4)
bullock   (l. 5)

2 Write the correct words in the pictures where indicated.

Close reading

Read the three extracts below and decide which one relates to picture B. Use any of the vocabulary above, which you should now understand, to help you decide.

Extract 2

In India water is often taken from a well using a hand pump. The water is usually clean and safe to drink. In some villages people use earthen jars that help to keep the water cool. The pump and the jars are made in India. They are the appropriate technology for the people.

Extract 3

In some villages in many developing countries people obtain their water from ponds close to the village. The water is not very clean but it is all they have. Women and children fill buckets or cans with water and carry it on their heads back to their homes. In some countries, such as Brazil, they make the water a little safer by passing it through a water filter. The pool, the can and the filter are simple and cheap and are suited to the way of life of the villages. For them it is an appropriate technology.

Extract 4

The water for the fields comes from a number of small ponds, or tanks as they are called in India, or from small streams. Specially made long troughs are dipped into the stream to scoop up water. The poles have heavy weights at the end and these act like balances to help lift up the long troughs so the water will flow out and into irrigation channels around the fields. It is the traditional way of irrigating in many parts of India and the troughs are made by the blacksmith in the village.

Inference: unfamiliar words

Find the words in extract 2 that mean:
a a machine for raising water
b a shaft sunk in the ground for obtaining water
c a utensil made of clay used to contain water

Word use: definitions

Write definitions for these words in extract 3:
             developing   filter   suited   appropriate
Try to use your own words: check with a dictionary if necessary.

Word use: synonyms

Find words in extract 4 which are similar in meaning to these:

        immersed   draw up   stabilizers   watering

Extraction of information

Look at pictures A and B and read extracts 1–4 again.

1 List the various methods of obtaining water.
2 Grade the methods in terms of cost, safety and appropriacy (use a scale of 1–10).
3 Taking information from the texts and pictures write a summary in your own words of how the Persian Wheel works.

Evaluation of the text

What do we learn from the text about appropriate technology?
Is a diesel or electric pump an example of appropriate technology? If not, why not?

Section B

Prediction

How to make a model of the Persian Wheel

Which of the following equipment would you expect to need to make a model of the Persian Wheel? Before you skim the diagram on page 87 for content, complete the first part of the table (I EXPECT TO NEED).

Equipment and tools	I EXPECT TO NEED		I NEED	
	YES	NO	YES	NO
a Various lengths of wood				
b A hammer				
c A chisel				
d Waterproof tape				
e Eighteen one-inch screws				
f Tins or cans				
g A ball of string				
h A bicycle wheel				
i A saw				
j A knife				
k A screwdriver				
l Wood glue				
m Scissors				
n Sheets of paper				
o A tin opener				

Skimming for content

Look briefly at the diagram on page 87 and see if your expectations are confirmed. Complete the second part of the table (I NEED).

Labelling a diagram

With reference to the chart on page 86, label all the
equipment and tools in the figure below.

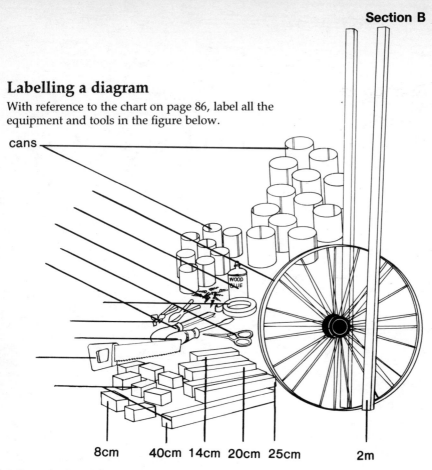

cans

WOOD GLUE

8cm   40cm 14cm 20cm 25cm   2m

Visual classification: illustrations to clarify instructions

1   Here are the first two instructions, a and b, of how to make a model of the
Persian Wheel. Read them carefully and study Figure 1. Then label Figure 2
so as to illustrate instruction b.

How to make the wheel

a   Fix the wooden blocks (F) to the edge of
the bicycle wheel with waterproof
tape. The tape must be wrapped right
around the block and the rim of the
wheel. (Fig. 1)

fig. 1

wheel rim

waterproof
tape

block of wood

spokes

8cm

b   Make sure each of the small cans has the
top properly removed (no sharp
edges) and has no holes in it. Attach the
cans to the blocks with the waterproof
tape and make sure they all face the same
way. This time the tape must be
wrapped right around the rim, the block
and the can. (Fig. 2)

fig. 2

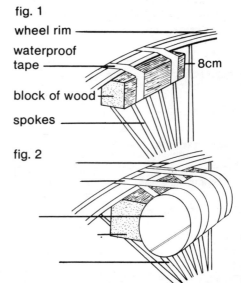

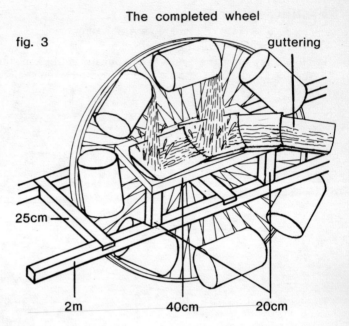

The completed wheel

fig. 3

guttering

25cm

2m   40cm   20cm

2   Here is a diagram (Figure 3) of the
completed Persian Wheel and a summary of
how to finish making it. Complete the
summary by referring to Figures 3 and 4.

After the wheel has been completed, the
support and guttering must be made. As
can be seen in Fig. 3 the support is
constructed from various lengths of ...[1]
The sides are made of the two long...[2]
pieces, supported by the two 25cm
lengths. The...[3] rests on a platform made
from the...[4] length of wood, glued and
screwed to the...[5] of the two 20cm pieces
which are fixed at right angles to one of
the...[6] lengths. The guttering (Fig. 4) is
made from...,[7] cut in...[8] lengthways. The
top half of one half-can is placed in the...[9]
of another half-can to complete the...[10]
Waterproof...[11] is run underneath the
gutter to join the...[12] together and to make the
gutter waterproof. It is then assembled on
the...[13] so that the centre of the...[14] on the
wheel are exactly above the centre of
the...[15] The wheel is placed in the
wooden...[16] with the cans on the same side
as the...[17]

Construction of the guttering

fig. 4

support

guttering

platform

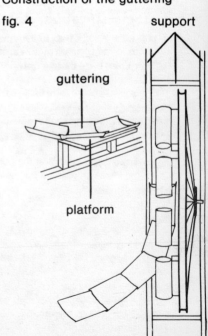

Section C

Anticipation

1   How many substances, such as paraffin and petrol, can you think of that are obtained from crude oil (that is, untreated oil taken straight from under the ground or sea)?

2   Make a list, placing the substances in order of importance.

Skimming for content

Read quickly through extract 1 and decide which of these titles fits best.

Refining Crude Oil

Crude Oil Extraction

Distilling Fractions

Extract 1

Crude oil is not a simple substance but a mixture of many different kinds of liquid. These useful liquids must be separated, and the separation process known as distillation is the first job of the oil refinery.

Distillation is what happens when a liquid is boiled, becomes a vapour, and is then condensed (or turned back into a liquid) by cooling it. The distillation of oil is complicated because crude oil is not one liquid but a mixture of several. Each of the liquids has its own boiling point, so that when crude oil is heated some parts of it boil and vaporise at low temperatures, others at higher temperatures, and some will boil only when the temperature is very high indeed. The vapours from these boiling liquids condense and change back into liquid form one after the other as soon as the temperature drops below the particular boiling point of each.

The distillation of crude oil in a refinery makes use of the fact that boiling and condensation take place at different temperatures with different liquids. The various liquids that together make up crude oil are known as fractions, and the process of distillation takes place in a tall steel tower called a fractionating column. The inside of the column is divided at intervals by a number of horizontal trays with holes in them. The column is kept very hot at the bottom but the temperature gradually falls towards the top, so that each tray is a little cooler than the one below it.

The fractions that rise highest in the column before condensing are called light fractions and those that condense on the lower trays are called heavy fractions. The very lightest fraction, taken off at the top of the column, is refinery gas, which remains a vapour and is used as fuel in the refinery. Other light fractions are gasoline (petrol) and naphtha (used in the chemical industry). A slightly heavier fraction is kerosine, which provides fuel for jet engines. Heavier again is gas oil, which is used as a fuel for diesel engines. From the base of the fractionating column is drawn off the residue, which contains the heaviest fractions of all, fuel oil and bitumen, both very important oil products. Bitumen is used for road surfacing and waterproofing, while fuel oils have a variety of uses in central heating, and in the production of ointments, polishes and lubricating oils.

Word use: word building

Find the nouns in the text which correspond with these verbs. Explain the meaning of the nouns as they are used in the text.

refine   mix   distil   condense   vaporize   separate

Visual classification: diagrams

1   Complete this diagram with words from the second paragraph.

Process of distillation

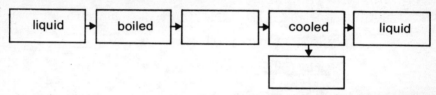

2   The information about fractions contained in the text could be classified in a diagram, either according to the various products of crude oil or according to the use of individual fractions. Study the diagram and complete it with information taken from the text.

Fractions from crude oil

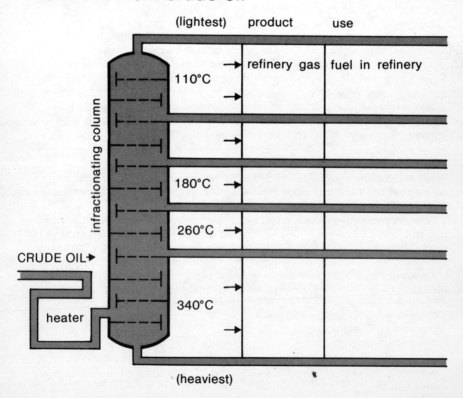

Summary

What is the method of refining crude oil? Complete the boxes below and write a short summary of the process.

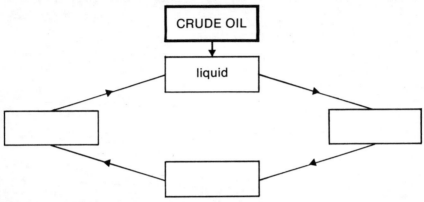

Close reading

1 Read the following text about the chemical products that can be produced from naphtha.

Extract 2

Naphtha, one of the light fractions obtained from the distillation column, is specially useful for the manufacture of chemicals. It can be broken down into a number of simple gases and liquids which are highly reactive; that is they combine readily with other substances to form new chemical compounds. They are therefore very useful 'building blocks' from which hundreds of chemicals can be manufactured. The variety of these chemical products is surprising.

Plastics have become some of the most useful of all man-made materials; and they are produced chiefly from oil-based chemicals. Many household articles can be made from plastic: bowls and buckets, cups, saucers and plates, television cabinets, chairs, toys, parts of refrigerators and washing machines, and many others.

Synthetic resins are used in many industries. Builders use them for wall and floor coverings, light fittings, pipes, plumbing, and insulation against the cold. The motor-car industry uses them for dashboards, steering wheels, car seats and interior fittings, and even for some engine parts.

Detergent powders and liquids, based on oil-based chemicals, are familiar to us in the home. Unlike natural soaps, they work in hard and soft water, and are very good for dissolving fat and grease. Similar detergents are very valuable in industry, particularly in the cleaning, dyeing and finishing of textiles.

Agricultural chemicals help the farmer to get the best yield of crops from his land in two different ways: by fertilising the soil and by killing weeds and pests. These fertilisers and pesticides have made the biggest contribution to agriculture, although insecticides are also important to keep farm animals healthy and to combat human disease.

Other types of chemicals made from oil include glycerine, used in the manufacture of drugs, foodstuffs, cosmetics and explosives; synthetic rubbers, essential to meet the world's demand for rubber; sulphur, for making sulphuric acid; and glycol for anti-freeze.

2 Complete the classification diagram below.

Chemicals from naphtha and their products

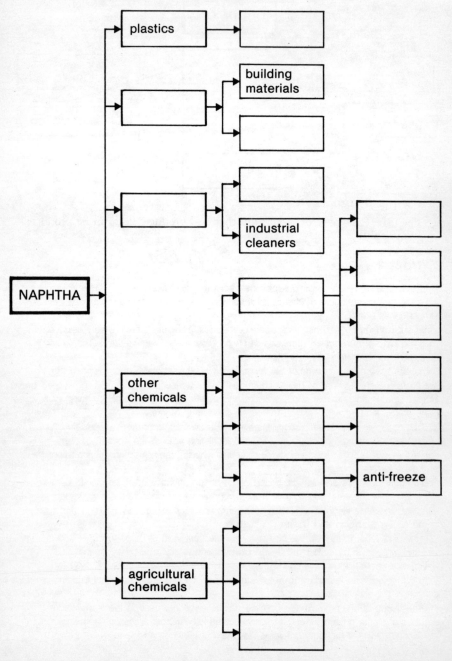

3 Produce a classification diagram showing the articles made from plastics –
(household articles, bowls, etc.). Add in the dotted box any other article that
you know is made from plastic material.

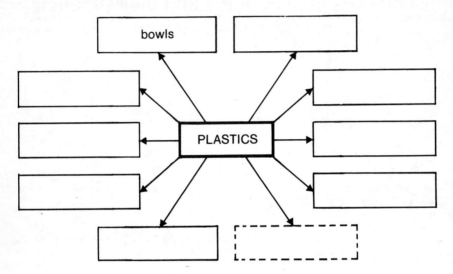

4 Choose one of the other naphtha chemicals and draw a classification diagram
showing the articles made from that naphtha product. Then write a short
paragraph about your chosen chemical, using information from your diagram.

Unit 9 **Literature**

Interpretation

In this unit all the reading skills, strategies and approaches dealt with throughout the book are used in the interpretation of the texts. Consideration must be given to the writer's intention, method and degree of success. Opinion regarding the last of these ultimately depends upon the reader's personal response to the text.

To respond personally, however, the reader needs not only to be sensitive to the aims and intentions of the writer but also to be aware of any underlying attitudes. Then, with reference to his or her own experience and background, the reader can interpret and respond to the writer's message.

There are three sections to this unit, employing contrasting texts which, however, are linked by the unifying theme of alienation.

Section A: A modern poem, in which the poet views aspects of ordinary life through the eyes of the ultimate alien, a visitor from another planet.

Section B: A famous Irish legend, in which the Celtic story-teller presents a view of heroic life of long ago, aspects of which may appear alien to the present-day reader.

Section C: A dramatic sketch, in which the playwright gives the reader an insight into a modern form of alienation.

Section A

Anticipation

Have you ever been to a country where the customs, behaviour, everyday objects, etc. were very different from those in your own country? What seemed most strange in that country? Did you write home and describe this? If not, consider how you might have described it. Think about physical objects, gestures, habits, the weather, the buildings, the food, etc.

Close reading

This poem by a contemporary English poet imagines how a visitor from the planet Mars might view everyday objects and activities.

First read the poem carefully. Do not worry if you can't understand everything the first time. This is quite normal with poetry, particularly in a foreign language!

A Martian Sends a Postcard Home

Caxtons are mechanical birds with many wings
and some are treasured for their markings—

they cause the eyes to melt
or the body to shriek without pain.

5 I have never seen one fly, but
sometimes they perch on the hand.

Mist is when the sky is tired of flight
and rests its soft machine on ground:

then the world is dim and bookish
10 like engravings under tissue paper.

Rain is when the earth is television.
It has the property of making colours darker.

Model T is a room with the lock inside –
a key is turned to free the world

15 for movement, so quick there is a film
to watch for anything missed.

But time is tied to the wrist
or kept in a box, ticking with impatience.

In homes, a haunted apparatus sleeps.
20 that snores when you pick it up.

If the ghost cries, they carry it
to their lips and soothe it to sleep

with sounds. And yet, they wake it up
deliberately by tickling with a finger.

 . . .

25 At night, when the colours die,
they hide in pairs

and read about themselves –
in colour, with their eyelids shut.

How many everyday objects and activities can you immediately identify?

Cohesion: discourse markers

There are seven subject areas in the poem. Mark these in your text, using the
punctuation, the division into stanzas, and the use of discourse markers and
reference to help you.

Cohesion: reference

What do these words refer to?

a one (l. 5)   d then (l. 9)
b they (l. 6)   e It (l. 12)
c its (l. 8)   f the ghost (l. 21)

Interpretation

1 Five everyday objects are described in the poem from an original point of view. They appear in the list of ten objects below. Give the line reference for each one. The first has been done for you. Find the other four.

books (lines 1–6)	car	clock	doorbell
plane	radio	table	telephone
toaster	watch		

2 Four everyday activities are similarly described. Look at the list of eight activities below and decide which four are in the poem. Give the line reference for each one.

crying	dreaming	eating	kissing
laughing	sleeping	thinking	writing

3 Explain how the poet uses metaphor in his descriptions. For example, consider the description of books (lines 1–6). (*Note:* Caxton was the first person to print books in England.) The poet likens books to birds, comparing the pages of a book to the wings of a bird, some of which are more highly valued than others for their markings (words and pictures). They can make the reader cry or laugh. When they are held in the hand, they look like birds perching there; but one thing they don't do is fly.

  Consider in the same way how the poet uses metaphor to describe:

  a mist   c a car
  b rain   d a telephone

4 Consider how the poet uses metaphor in his descriptions of everyday activities (see question 2).

Evaluation of the text

1 a Is this poem □ a narrative?
                    □ an argument?
                    □ a description?
   b Can you explain the title of the poem?

2 Is the poet successful in his descriptions? Which do you think works best? Are there any which you think are less effective? If so, why? What do you think of the poem?

3 Try to describe an everyday activity or object from a similarly original point of view.

SECTION B

Prediction

Read the introduction on page 97 and say whether you think the legend is likely to be a

tragedy   comedy   romance   satire

Give reasons for your choice.

Introduction

Some of the finest stories in the whole world are to be found amongst the ancient legends of Ireland. This first tale, one of 'The Three Sorrows of Storytelling', is probably the most famous of all Irish legends, and unhappy Deirdre has inspired Irish poets and writers for centuries.

Scanning

Answer these questions as quickly as possible while scanning extract 1.

1 Where in Ireland did Deirdre live?
2 What is the meaning of her name?
3 Who was Deirdre supposed to marry?
4 Where did Deirdre and the three brothers finally settle?

Extract 1

It was done as Conor said. The child was named Deirdre – Troubler – and in a house high in the hills, she was left in charge of three people only, two old servants, a man and a woman, and Lavarcham, Conor's poetess. And there, in that lonely place, Deirdre grew up into a lovely maiden.

5   When she was of an age for marriage, one winter morning, looking out through the window of the house with Lavarcham, Deirdre saw a pool of blood upon the snow, where the old man had killed a calf for their meal that day, and a raven alighting by it, to drink the blood.

'The man whom I wed,' said Deirdre, 'must have those three colours about him:
10   the colour of the raven for his hair, his skin the colour of the snow, and the colour of the blood upon his cheeks.'

Lavarcham smiled and answered thoughtlessly, 'There is but one man I know who is of those three colours. He is Naoise, the son of Usna, one of Conor's young warriors.'

15   'Bring him here to speak with me,' said Deirdre, 'for I shall not be happy until I have set eyes on him, if he is truly as you say.'

'Have you forgotten,' asked Lavarcham, regretting her words, 'that you are promised to the king?'

But Deirdre pleaded with her, and in the end she relented, thinking that there
20   could be little harm in one brief meeting, and she sent for Naoise. The eldest son of Usna was indeed as Lavarcham had said, with hair like the raven's wing, skin like snow, and cheeks as red as blood. And so far from there being no harm in a single meeting, the moment that they saw one another, Naoise and Deirdre fell in love.

'Never, never will I marry King Conor, now that I have seen you,' said Deirdre.
25   'Let us fly from here together.'

So Deirdre and Naoise and his two brothers, Ainnli and Ardan, with their men, fled from Ulster. But there was no one in all Ireland who would give them shelter, for fear of Conor's wrath; and after wandering from place to place, they crossed the sea to Scotland, and there the three brothers took service with the king. But even
30   then there was no peace for them, for the king of Scotland saw Deirdre and wished to have her for his wife, and would have slain Naoise to win her. So once again the sons of Usna were forced to flee. They went to one of the lonely islands off the western coast of Scotland, and there they lived in a little house which they had built themselves.

Close reading

1 Read extract 1 carefully and decide whether the raven is

a monster	a bird
an animal	a reptile

2 Say which of these elements are contained in extract 1.

a curse	a heroine
a hero	a battle
a rival	a death
a wish	an elopement

Word use: equivalents

Look at the expressions below and then find eight words in the text that have equivalent meanings.

killed	ran away
young woman	landing
anger	begged
marry	really

Why did the writer use those particular words in the text? Do you think these equivalent expressions convey the same feeling?

Interpretation

1 What is the purpose of including dialogue in the telling of the legend? Consider the effect of narration:

> Then Deirdre said the man she married must have
> three colours about him.

compared with direct speech:

> 'The man whom I wed,' said Deirdre, 'must have
> those three colours about him . . .'

Which is the more effective in the telling of the story? Find another example of dialogue in the text and consider its effectiveness.

2 Twice the colours red and white are mentioned, and the colour black implied, and likened to objects by the use of simile: 'as . . . as' or 'like'. Find three similes in the text. What do you think is the significance of colours in legends? For example, *Snow White and Rose Red* is the title of a well-known European fairy story, in which the colours white and red represent innocence and passion respectively. Can you find examples of colours in legends and fairy stories of your own country? Which colours are they?

3 Repeated reference to certain ideas or themes is a feature of the legend. Why do you think the colours are mentioned more than once? What is the purpose of this kind of repetition? Consider whether the legends were originally spoken or written. Find a further example of repetition in the extract.

4 There were three people in charge of Deirdre and three colours used in the description of the ideal man. Can you find another example of the use of the number three? Why was this number chosen, do you think, instead of another? Does it have any significance in legends of your own country?

Anticipation

Look back at the list of elements in question 2 of *Close reading*. Which would you expect to feature in the remainder of the legend?

Prediction

1 How do you expect the story to continue? Complete the first part of the table (I EXPECT).

	I EXPECT	I FOUND
a They lived happily ever after.		
b King Conor had his revenge.		
c Deirdre becomes the mother of three sons.		
d Naoise and Conor fight over Deirdre.		
e Naoise and his brothers are killed in battle.		
f Deirdre leaves Naoise and marries Conor.		
g Deirdre and Naoise die in the end.		

Now read extract 2 and see if your predictions were correct. Fill in the second part of the table (I FOUND).

Extract 2

. . . but Conor ordered them bound; and when it had been done, he called out, 'Who will slay these traitors for me?'

There was not one among the men of Ulster who would do so foul a deed for him; but a man from Norway, Maini of the Red Hand, stepped forward saying, 'I will do
5 it for you, lord.'

. . . Naoise said, 'My sword was given to me by Manannan Mac Lir, the sea god, and it never leaves a stroke unfinished. Let Maini use it and strike off all our heads at once.'

The three sons of Usna bent their necks close together, and Maini of the Red
10 Hand took up the sword and with one blow he struck off all three heads.

Deirdre flung herself down beside the dead brothers, tearing her golden hair in her grief; and she wept and spoke a lament over them.

'The three lions of the hill are dead,
The three sons of a king who ever made strangers welcome.

15 The three hawks of Slieve Gullion,
The three sons of a king who were served by many warriors.

It was joy to be with Naoise and Ainnli and Ardan,
My life will not last long now that they are gone.

O you who dig the grave for the sons of Usna,
20 Let it be wide and deep enough, that I may lie beside them.'

Then her heart broke and she lay down by Naoise and died.

2 Read the end of extract 1 and the beginning of extract 2 again; you will notice that they do not run consecutively. What do you think happened between the two extracts?

Interpretation

1   The story features a magical effect in extract 2: what is it and why do you think it is included?

2   Different emotions and emotional responses are portrayed in the legend, for example, 'Conor's wrath'. Find and name another three emotions in extract 2.

3   Before Deirdre dies, she speaks a lament. What animals are mentioned and why? What appears four times? What effect does the lament have?

Evaluation of the text

The story-teller uses various devices in the relating of the legend: mention of certain colours, repetition, simile, the lament. Which do you think is the most effective? Give reasons for your choice.

Section C

Skimming for content

Look quickly over the sketch below and answer these questions:

1   Where is the scene set?
2   How many characters are there?
3   How many characters actually speak?

REQUEST STOP

(*Note*: In London there are two types of bus stop: a bus is obliged to stop at the first type, but at the other, called a Request Stop, it only has to stop if a waiting passenger puts out his or her arm.)

A queue at a Request Bus Stop. A WOMAN *at the head, with a* SMALL MAN *in a raincoat next to her, two other* WOMEN *and a* MAN.

5   WOMAN [*to* SMALL MAN]: I beg your pardon, what did you say?

Pause.

All I asked you was if I could get a bus from here to Shepherds Bush.

Pause.

Nobody asked you to start making insinuations.

10 *Pause.*

Who do you think you are?

Pause.

Huh. I know your sort, I know your type. Don't worry, I know all about people like you.

15 *Pause.*

We can all tell where you come from. They're putting your sort inside every day of the week.

Pause.

All I've got to do is report you, and you'd be standing in the dock in next to no time.

20 One of my best friends is a plain clothes detective.

Pause.

I know all about it. Standing there as if butter wouldn't melt in your mouth.* Meet you in a dark alley it'd be . . . another story. [*To the others, who stare into space.*] You heard

what this man said to me. All I asked him was if I could get a bus from here to Shepherds
25   Bush. [*To him.*] I've got witnesses, don't you worry about that.

Pause.

Impertinence.

Pause.

Ask a man a civil question he treats you like a threepenny bit. [*To him.*] I've got better
30   things to do, my lad, I can assure you. I'm not going to stand here and be insulted on a
public highway. Anyone can tell you're a foreigner. I was born just around the corner.
Anyone can tell you're just up from the country for a bit of a lark. I know your sort.

Pause.

She goes to a LADY.

35   Excuse me, lady. I'm thinking of taking this man up to the magistrate's court, you heard
him make that crack, would you like to be a witness?

The LADY *steps into the road.*

  LADY: Taxi . . .

She disappears.

40 WOMAN: We know what sort she is. [*Back to position.*] I was the first in this queue.

Pause.

Born just round the corner. Born and bred. These people from the country haven't the
faintest idea of how to behave. Peruvians. You're bloody lucky I don't put you on a charge.
You ask a straightforward question—

45   *The others suddenly thrust out their arms at a passing bus. They run off left after it. The*
WOMAN, *alone, clicks her teeth and mutters. A man walks from the right to the stop, and
waits. She looks at him out of the corner of her eye. At length she speaks shyly, hesitantly,
with a slight smile.*

Excuse me. Do you know if I can get a bus from here . . . to Marble Arch?

* 'as if butter wouldn't melt in your mouth'. This expression means that a person (in this case the small man)
appears to be completely harmless and mild (although that person may well *not* be like that).

Close reading

Read the text carefully. Decide if these statements are true (T), false (F), or if it is
impossible to say (I), and mark them accordingly.

	T	F	I
a The woman wants to go to Shepherds Bush.			
b The small man never speaks to the woman.			
c The small man doesn't live in London.			
d The lady doesn't wait for a bus to come.			
e Everybody at the bus stop is waiting for a bus.			

a The woman wants to go to Shepherds Bush.
b The small man never speaks to the woman.
c The small man doesn't live in London.
d The lady doesn't wait for a bus to come.
e Everybody at the bus stop is waiting for a bus.

Interpretation

1 Consider the answers to these questions.
   a How do you think the woman started her conversation with the small
     man, and in what manner?
   b How does she think the small man replied to her question?
   c The woman talks about 'your sort . . . your type'. What sort or type
     does she mean?

d The woman says, 'We can all tell where you come from. They're putting your sort inside every day of the week.' Where does she imagine the man has come from? What does she mean by 'inside'?

e The woman says, 'Anyone can tell you're a foreigner. I was born and bred just around the corner.' What does she mean by this? Are there any other references in the sketch to this idea?

f The woman says, 'We know what sort she is.' What sort does she mean?

2 What is the implication behind these stage directions?

a *Pause.*
b *. . . the others, who stare into space.*
c *The* LADY *steps into the road.*

Evaluation of the text

1 What sort of person do you think the woman is? How do you picture her in terms of appearance, age and character?

2 a Is the language used here matter-of-fact or elaborate?
b Why did the writer choose to use this type of language?
c Is this sketch really just about a woman asking about the buses?
d What is the writer trying to say? How does he use humour to help him?
e Have you ever met a person like this? If so, what happened and how did you react?

Reading list

Unit 2 **Community**

Sully, Jessica, 'Boat People Adrift in London', LAM (London's Alternative Magazine).
An article about the plight of the Vietnamese refugees who have settled in Britain and found themselves cut off from their native culture and community life.

Steinbeck, John, *The Grapes of Wrath*, Heinemann, 1939.
A classic novel set during the economic depression in America in the 1920s. Many farmers were forced to leave their farms in the East and became migrant workers in the vineyards of California. This is the story of the deprivations of a dispossessed community struggling to survive in an alien state.

Harrison, Harry, *Make Room! Make Room!*, Doubleday, 1966, Penguin, 1967.
A science fiction story set in the near future, filmed as *Soylent Green*. The year is 1999, and the world is vastly overcrowded and community life has broken down. The starving people of America rely on soylent green, a kind of biscuit, for survival, but are unaware that it is made from recycling the dead.

Unit 3 **Travel**

Wade Labarge, Margaret, *Medieval Travellers*, Hamish Hamilton, 1982.
A scholarly but readable account of travel in the Middles Ages.

Theroux, Paul, 'Subterranean Gothic', *Granta 10: Travel Writing*, Granta Publications Ltd, 1984.
A classic piece of writing on the New York subway, one of a collection of pieces, both fact and fiction, by some of the best travel writers of the day.

Unit 4 **Language**

Spender, Dale, *Man Made Language*, Routledge & Kegan Paul, 1980.
A stimulating account of how language is created by and for men, and how women are placed at a disadvantage by the words we use.

Hudson, R. A., *Sociolinguistics*, Cambridge University Press, 1980.
A standard textbook on the relationship between language and society.

Unit 6 **Psychology**

Storr, Anthony, *Human Aggression*, Allen Lane, 1968.
A classic psychological exploration, very readable.

Roth, David, 'Pleasure Machine', *Omni*, Vol. 3, No. 4, 1980.
An interesting article on psychological research carried out at Ohio State University into defining and measuring pleasure.

Unit 7 **Art**

Berger, John, *Ways of Seeing*, Penguin Books, 1972.
The book of the acclaimed B.B.C. television series. A classic exposé of the way we look at art, and the way our looking is conditioned by historical circumstance, written from a polemical (Marxist) stance.

Procacci, Ugo, 'The technique of mural paintings and their detachment', in the Arts Council catalogue to the exhibition *Frescoes in Florence*, Hayward Gallery, 1969.
The catalogue to a major exhibition of Florentine frescoes.

Unit 8 **Technology**

Mister, Robert, *What is Appropriate Technology?*, Oxfam Education Department, 1979.
An information booklet describing appropriate technology and its application in the Third World. The focus is on life in Indian villages and the technology most compatible with the villagers' lifestyle. The Persian Wheel is one of the best ways of obtaining water for many of the villages.

Shell International Petroleum Co. Ltd, *Oil for Everybody*, 1968.
A handbook on the history of oil showing how it is formed below the earth or sea, how it is found, and the technology necessary to drill for it, extract it and refine it. The role of the oil companies, and in particular Shell, in finding and developing new products from oil, is also considered.

Unit 9 **Literature**

Raine, Craig, *A Martian Sends a Postcard Home*, Oxford University Press, 1979.
One of the best collections of contemporary poetry.

Picard, Barbara Leone, *Hero Tales from the British Isles*, Heinemann, 1963.
'Deirdre and the Sons of Usna', one of 'the three sorrows of storytelling', is probably the most famous of Irish legends. Three of Ireland's greatest writers, Yeats, Synge and James Stephens, have all written their versions of Deirdre's tragedy. The original story was written in the ninth century by an unknown Irish writer.

Pinter, Harold, *Request Stop*, Methuen, 1961.
One of the several review sketches by this famous playwright. Classic plays include *The Birthday Party*, *The Caretaker*, *Old Times* and more recently *Betrayal*.

Key

Unit 1 **Animals**

Section A

Skimming for content

2 a8 b4 c9 d13 e10 f1 g11 h12 i2 j6 k14 l3 m5 n7 o15

Skimming for text-type, function and tone

This is a suggested list of answers. There may be some variation of opinion.

text	1	2	3	4	5	6	7	8	9	10	11	12	13	14	15
text-type	a	a	a	d	f	a	g	a	a	b	c	e	a	a	e
function	f	b	b	a	h	b	h	b	b	c	e/d	c	b	b	g
tone	b	a	a	a	a	b	a	a	b	c	a	c	a	a	c

Scanning

1 The Explorers' Club
2 £1
3 Dead Dog Records
4 Wednesday night
5 Hamlet
6 400 million
7 Because there is a build-up of reproducing mussels on the oil rig legs
8 A prehistoric horse-like creature
9 Newts
10 1911
11 Because they breed quickly.
12 The rats that originally wiped out the puffin population have been exterminated.
13 1961
14 HRH The Prince of Wales
15 Franklin Watts

Section B

Skimming

1 First article
   content: the collared peccary has not been adopted by the public because of its ugliness.
   function: to report news.
   tone: half-neutral/half-humorous.
   Second article
   content: how the situation has changed thanks to the newspaper article.
   function: to report news.
   tone: half-neutral/half-humorous

2 i c
   ii a, c

3 a is the fourth paragraph of the second article
   b is the third paragraph of the first article
   c is the third paragraph of the second article

Scanning

1 Whipsnade Park Zoo
2 *The Observer*
3 South America
4 Mrs Anne Mead

Section C

Skimming for content 1

2 1d 2b 3c 4a 5b

Skimming for content 2
This is a suggested list of answers. There may be some variation of opinion.
1 a Y   b DK
2 c N   d L   e DK
3 f P   g P   h DK   i P
4 j L   k L   l DK
5 m L   n N
6 o Y   p L   q L   r Y
7 s N   t Y

Unit 2 **Community**

Section A

Previewing using titles and headings
1 a Opposition to plans for a new town. A new town to be built in the country is on the drawing board but there are doubts about its realization.
  b A housing estate with a lot of young couples/A caring community/A place where love dwells.
  c A humorous look at an otherwise dull or serious subject/A situation which would be impossible without humour or jokes.
  d The problems of Vietnamese refugees in London/Stranded sailors or fishermen in London.
  e Travelling folk/Gypsies and tinkers.
  f A farming community/Vineyards/A novel about the countryside, farmers and vintners – anger involved.
  g The problems of young people today/Disturbed children.
  h An adventure with a despairing ending/People and/or ships that have lost their way.

2 1b   2d   3e   4h   5a   6g   7c   8f

3 a   b   d   f   h

Previewing using blurbs
1f   2e   3d   4c   5h   6b   7g   8a

Previewing using a table of contents
Downwave is about the decline of society.
Chapters 5 and 6 have helpful headings and even more helpful sub-headings.
Pages vii, 1, 8, 14–16, 19, 20, 27, 33–42, 48, 52–53, 63, 74 and 78–97 could provide further clarification of the book's subject matter.

Previewing using illustrations
1 Asian children, who are sad, lonely, abandoned, bewildered.
2 Homeless in Another Culture/Sad and Far from Home/What Am I Doing Here?
3 d

Section B

Prediction: the ends of sentences
1 . . . have made life difficult for them.
2 . . . they could turn for support.
3 . . . housing, employment and social pressures.
4 . . . Singapore and Hong Kong.
5 . . . help the 'boat people'.
6 . . . take increasing responsibility for the refugees.
7 . . . deal with crises
8 . . . the flats are hard to get.
9 . . . they are finding work hard to come by
10 . . . isolated and dependent.
11 . . . few jobs available anyway.

Anticipation
a   d

Close reading
a   d   c

Scanning
1   He's a policeman.
2   Times Square, New York.
3   In case there is a riot.
4   31 December, 1999.

Close reading
a F   b T   c T   d T

Word use: synonyms
joker: comedian   milling: restless   precinct: district   nut cults: religious sects

Prediction: the continuation of a story
1   b Reasons: It's too cold to riot.
              There are not many people there.
2   d follows immediately, then b   e   a   c

Anticipation
a P   b L   c L   d U   e L   f U
Possible endings to the story:
Steve gets involved with Shirl again (happy ending).
Steve doesn't get involved with Shirl again (unhappy ending).
Society continues to deteriorate (violent ending).
Life drifts on much as usual (inconclusive ending).
In fact it ends ironically with words on the giant screen:

CENSUS SAYS UNITED STATES HAD BIGGEST YEAR

EVER END OF CENTURY

344 MILLION CITIZENS IN THESE GREAT UNITED STATES

HAPPY NEW CENTURY!

HAPPY NEW YEAR!

Evaluation of the text
verbs of sound: stamping, grunted, screaming, cheered, shouted, ticked, shrieked, talking
verbs of movement: stamping, pointed, chased, glanced, slipped, worked (his way), pressed, washed, flicked, flying, breaking up, moved away, cleared (a space), come in, line up, lit up, passed by, came out, emerged, moved, head off, starting, turned back

Unit 3 **Travel**

Section A

Skimming for text-type
c

Prediction
I FOUND: a No   b Yes   c No   d No

Scanning
1   Chancellor of England
2   France
3   About two hundred

Close reading
a False   b True   c False   d True   e False

Section B

Skimming for content
1a about an underground railway
 b fact
2a True
 b True

Inference: unfamiliar words
a scalping (l. 14)
b a plain-clothes man (l. 28)
c mug (l. 30)
d i slap (l. 30)
   ii punch (l. 33).

Inference: implied meaning
1a The streets have numbers not names. The degree of violence. The police are armed. The underground railway is called a 'subway'. The Italian and Dutch surnames (Minucci and Haag), which indicate a racial mix.
 b To travel safely.
 c Because it is dirty and unpleasant.
 d Subway stops under the streets with the same numbers.
 e Very.
 f Because 'Her wristwatch was exposed and her handbag dangled from the arm closest to the door.'
 g Because they preferred to watch her and possibly catch a mugger in the act.
 h 1 Keep away from isolated cars (l. 7).
     2 Never display jewellery (ll. 8–9).
     3 Don't sit next to the door (l. 15).
     4 Keep near the conductor and the man in the token booth (ll. 18–20).
     5 At night keep near the token booth until the train comes in (l. 20–21).
     6 Stay with the crowds (l. 22).
     7 Keep away from quiet stairways (l. 22).
     8 Don't ride the subway if you don't have to (l. 41–2).
2 i c   d
   ii c

Word use: synonyms
    riding: travelling   subway: underground   car: carriage
    swell: great   conductor: guard

Unit 4 Language

Section A

Anticipation
1 & 2 (*Note:* The words marked ♀ are typically applied to women only, but this application is by no means universal or laudable.)

address	announce	argue	♀ bitch
chat	♀ chatter	complain	debate
declaim	declare	discuss	dispute
drone	explain	gabble	♀ gossip
grumble	harangue	mention	♀ nag
narrate	♀ natter	negotiate	♀ prattle
preach	pronounce	recite	remark
say	speak	utter	waffle
♀ whine	whisper		

Key

Skimming for function, text-type and content
  i a
  ii b
  iii c

Close reading
I FOUND: a Yes b Yes c Yes, if you accept the mention of tape recordings as evidence. d. No e Yes. These are implied, e.g. in the comments on the time imbalance in recorded conversations between men and women, in the section on giving new meanings to old words, and in the last paragraph.

Inference: unfamiliar words
irrefutable: cannot be disproved, very strong and clear
hogging: taking too much for oneself
termagant: a noisy, quarrelsome woman
enshrine: put in a holy place (a shrine), sanctify
hassle: fuss, argument

Word use: lexical sets

	M	F	∅	−
i say	✓	✓	✓	−
reply	✓	✓	✓	−
speak	✓	✓	✓	−
call oneself	✓	✓	✓	−
chatter	−	✓	−	✓
natter	−	✓	−	✓
prattle	−	✓	−	✓
nag	−	✓	−	✓
bitch	−	✓	−	✓
whine	−	✓	−	✓
gossip	−	✓	−	✓
express	✓	✓	✓	−

	M	F	+	−
ii king	✓	−	✓	−
queen	✓	✓	✓	✓
sir	✓	−	✓	−
dame	−	✓	−	✓
master	✓	−	✓	−
mistress	−	✓	−	✓
courtier	✓	−	✓	−
courtesan	−	✓	−	✓

Cohesion: reference
Chatter natter prattle nag bitch whine . . .

Dale Spender has a theory that the spoken word is heavily spiked with male chauvinism. Sally Adams reports.

Men interrupt women more than women interrupt men. Men talk more than women. These simple theories go against received/perceived wisdom but they are easy to demonstrate in any mixed group.

Test them out at your next dinner party. Staff meetings or work conferences are not recommended for beginners; social occasions are safer.

Dale Spender believes the male muscle in linguistics is irrefutable and has hundreds of tape recordings to prove it. Her research has convinced her that a whole new approach to language study is needed and this has not endeared her to male academic colleagues.

She's tenacious, persistent and annoying. One man said: 'You make a problem every time we talk.'

'Now you know what it's like,' she replied.

The problem is not solved by exposing it. For her it's a continuing struggle to get in her 50 per cent's worth. Even when she thinks she's been hogging the conversation, scrutiny afterwards shows she spoke only around 30 per cent.

She won't be manipulated. 'They can't use "bitch" to pull me into line as they could have done when I was 25.' She's 37. 'Instead of pushing me back into my place, it serves as a reinforcement. When someone says, "You're a bitch" I know I'm doing the right thing.'

Sounds like a termagant? A front-line stormtrooper in the monstrous regiment? She's a feminist but calls herself a 'closet heterosexual'. She's been living with the same fellow for six years.

'Most of my friends haven't met him. I've no wish to make him an honorary woman.' Every morning she cooks his breakfast. 'It's my vulnerability . . . But I do it because it's not expected of me.' Men who live with feminists are very special, she says.

She's an Australian, with plenty of degrees and diplomas, who teaches women's studies at the Institute of Education, University of London, edits *Women's Studies International Quarterly*, and writes. She's currently working on *Women of Ideas*, a book about the buried generations of women thinkers. *Man Made Language* is published on Thursday. Men, she says, have encoded words and these contain an inherent bias to silence women and enshrine male supremacy.

She's a passionate egalitarian, appalled by statistics like: women do four-fifths of the world's work, earn one-tenth of the world's salaries, and own 1 per cent of the world's wealth.

How does this relate to language? To her it's all about power. Consider male and female titles and how the female ones have been downgraded. King OK, queen now has added homosexual meanings; sir OK, dame has pantomime links; master OK, mistress overt sexual meanings; courtier OK, courtesan now only sexual meanings.

Why is there no word for man talk equivalent to chatter, natter, prattle, nag, bitch, whine and gossip? Why is there no four-letter shock word for rape as there is for sexual intercourse? Rape is a respectable safe word, perfectly acceptable in polite conversation. There's no taboo word to express the force, the trauma of rape. Why? Could it be because the victim's experience is outside male awareness?

Dale says because men encoded the language, it is deficient for women's meanings. There is no word, she says, which expresses being in the wrong just because you're a woman. 'There's no word that sums up the fact that you start from a position of not being an authority, not even on yourself.'

Key

Sometimes old words are given new meanings. Spinning, for instance, used to rep-
→ resent the journey feminists are making and is taken from spinster, evoking the whirling
movement of creation.

Academics attack her, saying this is not linguistics, but that, she says emphatically
triumphantly, is just her point. Linguistics is a male study of the language encoded by
→ men. They have this notion, she says, that they can say things more quickly and say
them better. But they are saying what words mean to them.

She started her research into language and sex 'by doing stupid things like counting
adjectives. Then I realized I had to look at people s assumptions.

'Why do they think women's language is deficient? Why was there a big hassle about
women announcers on the BBC? Who talks more? Who interrupts?'

Her credo is now clear. 'We need a language which constructs the reality of women's
autonomy, women's strength, women's power. With such a language we will not be a
muted group.'

Spender, Dale, *Man Made Language*, Routledge & Kegan Paul.

Cohesion: ellipsis
i 'Now you know what problems women have with language,' she replied. 'There is a
problem in every conversation, every sentence even.'
ii her 50 per cent's worth of the conversation.
iii The word 'master' is OK, but the word 'mistress' has overt sexual meanings.
iv The word 'courtier' is OK, but the word 'courtesan' now has only sexual meanings.

Summary
In this interview Dale Spender talks about *her* work researching the *male* dominance of
language. *She* believes, *and can prove*, that language was created by men, for men. For this
reason *she* is *un*popular with *her* male academic colleagues. *She asserts, and can prove*, that
men talk much more than *women*. *She* asks why so many words that describe *female* character
and activity should have negative meanings. Finally, *she* believes that language should be
changed to reflect the experience of women more fairly.

Extraction of information
The jacket blurb might read something like this:

Dale Spender, an Australian by birth, teaches Women's Studies at the Institute of Education, University of London. She edits *Women's Studies International Quarterly*, and writes.
She is currently working on *Women of Ideas*, a book about the buried generations of women
thinkers. As a feminist, Dale Spender is involved with the present inequality of women.

Dale Spender is 37 years old and unmarried.

Section B
Skimming for content
a The third paragraph
b The second paragraph

Scanning
1 Along the north-west Amazon, half in Brazil and half in Colombia.
2 About the size of England.
3 About 10,000.
4 Tukano.
5 Long-houses.

Word use: definitions
exogamous e   patrilocal c
lingua franca d   phratry b
patrilingual a

110

Close reading
1 a T b F c T d F e T f T
2 c

Cohesion: discourse markers
1 now
2 though
3 Geographically
4 but
5 in turn
6 First
7 The second fact is that
8 It is perhaps worth pointing out that
9 thus
10 Putting these two facts together
11 We now add a third fact
12 not only . . . but also
13 but rather
14 as though
15 thus
16 so
17 Indeed
18 so

Unit 5 **Advertising**

Section A

Skimming for content
1 Nursing (particularly psychiatric nursing) as a career.
2 What the difference is between normal and abnormal behaviour.
 How an RMN can help the mentally disturbed, both children and adults.
 Nursing the mentally disturbed is not exactly what people traditionally think it is.
 It's a difficult but rewarding job.

Scanning
1 Registered Mental Nurse
2 Three years
3 Bosch's art
 The man dressed as a bumble-bee.
 Brian's obsession
 In adults, obsessive behaviour (e.g. continually rearranging cups on a table) and perhaps depression, anxiety and thoughts of suicide.

Inference: unfamiliar words
unravelled: deciphered, made clear, taken to pieces to understand better
bagpipes: musical instrument consisting of a bag and pipes (as found in Scotland)
weird: strange
bumble-bee: a large, loud-humming bee (a type of insect) striped black and yellow
tantrums: attacks of bad temper which are fierce and uncontrolled
overwhelming: overpowering, out of all proportion
on the brink of: on the edge of
wards: rooms in the hospital where patients sleep and live

Word use: varieties of meaning
i The meaning most people would attach to this word is similar to that conveyed by such words as 'ordinary', 'typical', 'usual', 'acceptable'. The inverted commas suggest that this is an unusual interpretation of the word and that there can equally well be other meanings.
ii Because this is a popular term which has acquired negative or derogatory overtones. Consequently the professionals prefer not to use it.
iii mad (l.9): suffering from severe, perhaps incurable, brain disorder
 mentally disturbed (l.9): not as severe as 'mad', the balance of the mind has been upset but could be righted
 different (l.11): not wanting to be 'normal'
 abnormally (l.20): the opposite of normally
 an obsession (l.36): a clinical condition characterized by the fixation of the mind on an object or a particular kind of behaviour
 mentally ill (l.77): not mentally 'normal', e.g. mad, mentally disturbed

Text analysis 1: discourse at sentence level

1 a describing: 'The man is balancing a tray on top of his head. On the tray is a set of pink bagpipes.' (ll.3–4)
   b reporting: 'When he was three, Brian and his teddy bear were inseparable.' (l.30)
   c generalizing: 'Most children go through a phase like this.' (l.33)
   d exemplifying: ' . . . unnecessary things, like continually rearranging cups on a table.' (ll.71–2)
   e explaining: '(an RMN never expects quick results)'. (ll.60–61)
   f stating a cause: ' . . . his wife leaving him'. (l.74)
   g stating a result: 'Later he could spend a whole day without his companion and go to school alone.' (ll.64–5)
   h stating a contrast: 'However, if instead of his usual shirt and tie, the man started to turn up at work every morning dressed as an insect . . .' (ll.25–7)
   i asking a rhetorical question: 'In particular, what do we mean by "normal"?' (l.16)
   j answering a rhetorical question: 'We'll never really know.' (l.12)
   k inviting the reader to do something: 'Let's consider Brian, now seven years old.' (l.29)
   l making a suggestion to the reader: 'Perhaps nursing the mentally ill isn't a job you'd normally think of yourself doing.' (ll.77–8)
   m instructing the reader to do something: 'For more information, write to the Chief Nursing Officer.' (ll.105–6)

2 Where the introduction ends is open to discussion. The point of it is to give a famous example of someone who, depending on your point of view, might or might not have been mad, mentally disturbed, abnormal, etc. It functions as an example which then leads into the question 'what do we mean by "normal"?'. The intention is to show how difficult it is to answer that question. The introduction could end, therefore, after these difficult questions have been asked (l.20) or after the example of Bosch but before the questions (l.14).

ll. 1–4	describing
ll. 5–11	asking rhetorical questions
l. 11	answering rhetorical questions
ll. 12–14	reporting *or* explaining
l. 15	stating a result
ll. 16–20	asking rhetorical questions

Style
informal, in order to involve the reader

Extraction of information
Qualities:
'an immense calmness and understanding' (ll. 54–5)
patience – 'an RMN never expects quick results' (ll. 60–61)
'enormous skill' (l. 68)
'a great deal of intelligence and imagination' (ll. 69–70)

Job information:
'part of a highly professional team' (ll. 55–6)
'It's by no means a "normal" job' (l. 79)
not a normal 'nine-to-five' job (ll. 81–2)
most of the time spent in the community rather than in wards (ll. 90–91)
three-year training involving hospital and community experience, practical assessment and tough written exams (ll. 99–101)
challenging and provoking – 'introduces you to qualities in yourself you might never normally have discovered' (ll. 103–4)

Section B
Close reading
1d   2c   3e   4a   5f   6b

Inference: unfamiliar words
ransacked: searched through roughly, turned upside down by someone trying to find
  something
brawl: noisy argument and fight in a public place
step in: intervene
rise above: get under control, learn to ignore

Text analysis 1: discourse at paragraph level
f   d   a   h   b   c   g   e

Style
informal

Evaluation of the text
wanted by the police: The police want to question the person concerned in relation to a
  crime. Here, though, it merely means they want new recruits.
on the beat: A policeman 'on the beat' is on duty, patrolling certain streets assigned to him.
bring you in for questioning: This is what the police do when they arrest you on suspicion
  of committing a crime. Here it merely means to give you an
  interview.

Section C

Skimming for content
1 It is about advertising standards and controls, and the right of the public to be involved.
   The picture illustrates how advertisements can distort and misrepresent reality.
2 a3   b5   c1   d4   e2

Scanning
1 500
2 No. The IBA is responsible for these.
3 Because it can't monitor every advertiser all the time.
4 Over 7,500.
5 No. First it asks advertisers to back up their claims with solid evidence.
6 The advertising business, in order to make sure the system of self-control worked in the
   public interest.
7 'If an advertisement is wrong, we're here to put it right.'

Inference: unfamiliar words
play fair with: act in a fair way with
pledging: making a solemn promise
akin to: similar to
seedlings: young plants (newly grown from seed)
yardstick: measuring device
gauge: measure
circulars: printed advertising material sent by post
breach: disobey
sheer: absolute, pure (this word intensifies the following word)
monitor: keep an eye on
back up: support
amend: improve, rectify
contravenes: goes against
sceptical: distrusting, doubting
levy: a form of tax
prevail: win

Word use: antonyms
weakling: he-man
knowingly: unwittingly

Word use: word-play
1 They all exaggerate what they are advertising. For example:
    1 to turn you into a 15 stone he-man, rather than just build you up

2 to take years off your life, rather than just make you look a little younger
3 for seedlings suddenly to turn into 'a riot of colour'
4 '5 minutes walk from the beach' must mean just that
5 'Overlooking a river' is not the same as 'backing onto a ditch'
2 a Mr Universes flex their muscles in competitions. Here the ASA says it would do the same if an advertisement was misrepresentative, meaning it would prepare for a fight with the advertiser.
  b The metaphor is based on the idea of gardening. Weeds have to be pulled up by their roots. The extravagant ('flowery') prose of a misleading advertisement would have to be similarly eliminated.
  c This expression refers to showing someone the exit door, making them leave. The word-play comes from the fact that this section is to do with estate agents, who sell houses and as part of their job have to show clients round them.

Style
The text is fairly formal in its use of language. However, the word-play reduces the level of formality, and the sentences are generally short and direct. The text is also polite in its treatment of the subject matter and towards the reader.

Text analysis 1: discourse at whole-text level
i c   ii d   iii d   iv c   v b

Unit 6 **Psychology**

Section A

Skimming for content, text-type, function and tone
content: the natural aggression of children is inhibited for their own safety (or so we think); this leads later to psychological problems, e.g. frustration
text-type: a book on psychology
function: to present facts and to support them with evidence
tone: formal

Close reading
a True   b True   c False   d True   e False   f True

Word use: equivalants
characteristics: features
limited: curtailed
dangers: hazards
the extra parts, the accessories: the trappings
a high, steep rock facing the sea: a cliff
very steep, vertical: sheer
be bold enough to do something risky: venture
do something first, prepare the way for others: pioneer
inborn: innate
seize and hold: grasp
necessarily: perforce

Cohesion: reference and ellipsis
a dangers (l. 3)
b to guard them too carefully (l.7)
c to venture onto the glass (l.11)
d quite tiny children (ll. 15–16)
e to ride bicycles and use gymnasium equipment (l. 19)
f the obstruction of the life force in its development (l. 24)

Text analysis 2: cause and effect
paragraph 1
of the dangers that exist in the world around them.

traffic, electricity, gas and stairs.
As a result
we are forced to overprotect our children psychologically
because

they are ill-equipped to look after themselves when surrounded by the dangerous trappings of civilization.
paragraphs 2 and 3
the visual cliff experiment.
the Peckham Health Centre swimming experiment.

we can leave our children alone more than we do at the moment.
paragraph 4
frustration is caused in early childhood.

modern man is faced with the problem of aggression which has been repressed since
childhood.

Section B

Skimming for content
The Pleasure Machine: a comfortable seat which produces pleasurable sensations when a
button is pushed.

Scanning
1 Freud
2 Two decades (twenty years)
3 The pain seat
4 Stanley Milgram
5 Over 15 minutes

Word use: synonyms
1j   2f   3g   4a   5i   6d   7c   8k   9b   10l   11e   12h

Text analysis 2: contrast

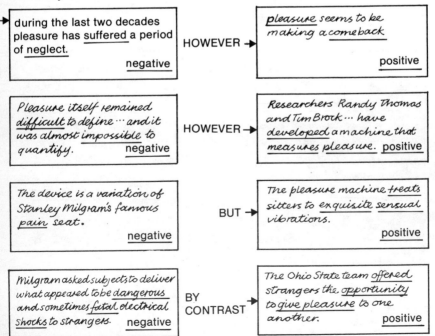

ET → | during the last two decades pleasure has <u>suffered</u> a period of <u>neglect</u>. negative | HOWEVER → | *pleasure seems to be making <u>a comeback</u>* positive |

| *Pleasure itself remained <u>difficult to define</u> ··· and it was almost <u>impossible to quantify</u>.* negative | HOWEVER → | *Researchers Randy Thomas and Tim Brock ··· have developed a machine that measures <u>pleasure</u>.* positive |

| *The device is a variation of Stanley Milgram's famous <u>pain</u> seat.* negative | BUT → | *The pleasure machine treats sitters to exquisite <u>sensual</u> vibrations.* positive |

| *Milgram asked subjects to deliver what appeared to be <u>dangerous</u> and sometimes <u>fatal</u> electrical shocks to strangers.* negative | BY CONTRAST → | *The Ohio State team <u>offered</u> strangers the <u>opportunity</u> to <u>give pleasure</u> to one another.* positive |

115

Section C

Prediction
a

Close reading
2 a False   b False   c True   d False   e False   f False   g True

Inference: implied meaning
1 In our society many people feel that to give or receive physical pleasure is somehow illicit and therefore 'dirty, immoral, and beneath their dignity'. This attitude is left over from the Victorian era when all physical pleasure was associated with sex and sensual pleasure did not exist in its own right.
2 This is to do with the master/servant syndrome and the class system which still exists. People who considered themselves inferior would try to please their superiors (often in the hope of better treatment, or gain, for themselves).
3 Because they were already emotionally involved and therefore took more pleasure in pleasing each other.
4 Probably because life is becoming more automated and many people feel dehumanized. More technical equipment is available to ease people's lives (labour-saving devices such as washing machines, spare people's hands), so why not spare your emotions with a pleasure machine?

Text analysis 2: comparison
1
social status:	'If, . . . more pleasure than others would.' (ll.15–18)
men:	'Men gave women more intense . . . other men.' (ll.20–22)
women:	'And women were just as conventional.' (ll.22–3)
	'They preferred . . . than for other women.' (ll.23–5)
men and women:	' . . . the more attractive the person, the more pleasure he or she received.' (ll.28–9)
couples:	' . . . pleasure giving works better with heterosexual pairs.' (ll.18–19)
	'Dating couples . . . all other twosomes.' (ll.40–42)
	' . . . the more intimately . . . willing to offer.' (ll.42–5)
	' . . . the best pleasure . . . interaction between people.' (ll.58–60)

Some _hedonists_... hogged more than 15 minutes of _absolute personal pleasure._   positive

HOWEVER → Then the scientists had _trouble_ persuading them to stand up and go home.   negative

...subjects _were allowed_ to give themselves the experience by pressing the button that set the seat vibrating.   positive

BUT → ... the question Brock and Thomas wished to address with their chair _wasn't_ self-satisfaction   negative

2
Evaluation of the text
Pain is not seen as 'dirty, immoral, and beneath [people's] dignity' whereas pleasure is by some.
Pleasure is linked with intimate pairings. A pleasurable sensation is not offered to strangers easily.
In 'rat-race' society, people are encouraged to climb to the top by any means available. This breeds insensitivity towards others, and people with this ruthless instinct are not too squeamish about inflicting pain on their fellow men.
Punishment is often seen as 'doing people good' whereas pleasure is seen as indulgence.

Unit 7 **Art**

Section A

Skimming for function and text-type
i b   ii d

Scanning
a Clark
b Clark
c Clark
d Clark
e Berger
f Berger
g Berger
h Berger
i Gowing
j Gowing (Hayman)
k Berger
l Berger
m Berger

Close reading
a6   b2   c4   d1   e5   f7   g3

Word use: dictionary use
disingenuousness: insincerity, dishonesty
poaching: killing or stealing game or fish
whipping: a beating with a stick, lash, etc.
enhanced: heightened, increased

Inference: unfamiliar words
1 proprietary: belonging to the proprietor (wealthy owner)
   stance: way of standing
   bedevils: has a bad effect on
   precludes: prevents
   deportation: being sent out of the country (refers to criminals)
2 mastery: control of his skill of painting and control of the subject-matter.
   direct: painting from life, i.e. a faithful representation of what he saw in front of
            him
   melodious: harmonious, his style suggesting a beautiful melody
   simple: unwise, uneducated
   affords: offers, presents
   uncorrupted: untouched, natural
   unperverted: in all its original goodness, before any human intervention
   render: show, create
   substantiality: the physical substance (and wealth) that their land contained, the
                    physicality of an idea

Section B

Anticipation
1 an oil painting: painting on canvas with oil-based paints
   a watercolour: painting on paper with water-based paints
   a drawing: creating a picture using pencil, charcoal, ink, etc.
   a print: reproducing a picture through the process of printing (using a printing press,
   stone, woodcut, etc.)
   a fresco: painting on fresh plaster, which dries the painting to the wall

Close reading
two types of plaster
red paint
a bunch of feathers
a thin solution of ochre
fine cord
charcoal
a small pointed brush
sinopia red

Word use: definitions
arriccio c
intonaco a
sinopia b

Word use: antonyms

even: rough/uneven
lower: upper
horizontal: vertical
blunt: pointed
strong: light/faint

unfinished: complete
disappear: come to light
slow-moving: rapid
detailed: summary
temporarily: permanently
rough: smooth

Word use: equivalents

stick: adhere
carried out: executed
fixed: fastened
tight: taut
straight: directly

rubbed out: erased
gone over: retraced
finished: complete
marks: traces
a lot of: numerous
forced: compelled

Close reading
a F   b F   c T   d T   e T   f F

Inference: implied meaning
1 That artists at that time had a different attitude to their work and felt that the artist was less exalted than later generations came to feel.
2 So that the smooth upper layer on which the fresco was executed would adhere properly to the wall.
3 So that he could easily sort out the proportions of the design of his fresco, and transfer it from his sketch if he had made one.
4 To fix the design to the wall.
5 Because frescoes have to be painted on wet plaster.
6 Seven.
7 Very, because they can now study the stages in the artistic process, as well as having a new art-form to appreciate.

Visual comprehension: text-response
1 Stage 5 (ll. 18–19)
2 Stage 6 simply involves going over the outline in red (*sinopia*).

Unit 8 **Technology**

Section A

Anticipation
a F   b T   c P   d T   e T

Scanning
1 The diesel pump   2 In the village   3 The bullock
4 The blacksmith   5 A waterwheel

Visual classification: illustrations to support a text
Picture A

Inference: unfamiliar words
1 trough: a long, narrow receptacle   bucket: a container, often for water
   stream: a small river   channel: a narrow passage for water
   bullock: young or castrated bull

2

A

steam   bullock   bucket   channel

trough

B

Close reading
Extract 4

Inference: unfamiliar words
a pump   b well   c earthen jar

Word use: definitions
developing: growing, advancing, getting economically stronger, richer
filter: a device for purifying water, for removing impurities
suited: suitable, appropriate
appropriate: right, suitable

Word use: synonyms
dipped   scoop up   balances   irrigating

Extraction of information

1 Scooping it up from streams with balancing troughs.
Using a Persian Wheel.
Taking it out of ponds with buckets or cans.
Drawing it up from wells.
Using pumps (electric and diesel).

2

Cost	Safety	Appropriacy	
1	10	5	buckets
3	7	4	buckets and filters
5	6	3	balancing troughs
7	5	2	Persian Wheel
10	3	9	pumps

Evaluation of the text

Appropriate technology is technology suitable for the people it serves. It should be cheap, safe to use, provide better conditions for the people, and be produced locally.
No, because it cannot be built in the villages and is expensive to buy and repair.

Section B

Skimming for content

I NEED:

a Yes b No c Yes d Yes e Yes f Yes
g No h Yes i Yes j No k Yes l Yes
m Yes n No o Yes

Labelling a diagram

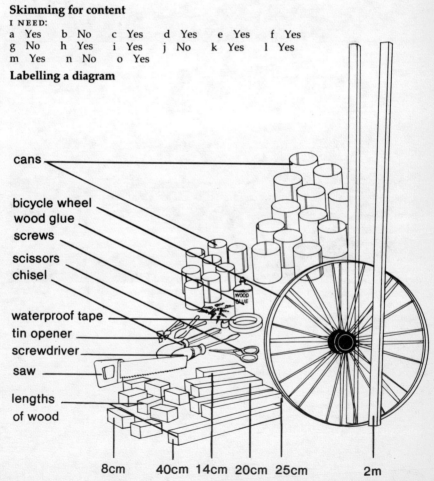

cans

bicycle wheel
wood glue
screws

scissors
chisel

waterproof tape
tin opener
screwdriver

saw

lengths
of wood

8cm   40cm 14cm 20cm 25cm   2m

Visual classification: illustrations to clarify instructions

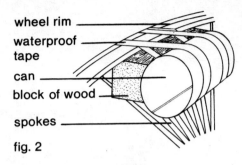

wheel rim

waterproof tape

can

block of wood

spokes

fig. 2

1	wood	7	cans	13	platform
2	2m	8	half	14	cans
3	guttering	9	bottom	15	guttering
4	40m	10	guttering	16	support
5	top	11	tape	17	guttering
6	2m	12	cans		

Section C

Anticipation
This is a suggested list of answers.

petrol

refinery gas

gas oil

fuel oil

paraffin

naphtha

diesel oil

bitumen

(gasoline and kerosine are other names for petrol and paraffin)

Skimming for content
Refining Crude Oil

Word use: word building
refinery: place where crude oil is refined
mixture: combination of several liquids
distillation: process of separating liquids which are mixed together
condensation: process of cooling a vapour to turn it back into a liquid
vapour: a liquid when boiled
separation: dividing one liquid from another

1 Visual classification: diagrams

Process of distillation

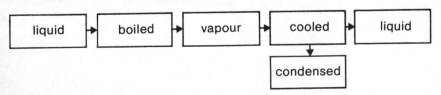

2 Fractions from crude oil

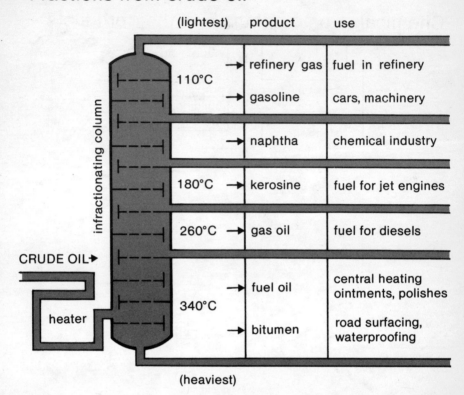

	(lightest)	product	use
110°C		→ refinery gas	fuel in refinery
		→ gasoline	cars, machinery
		→ naphtha	chemical industry
180°C		→ kerosine	fuel for jet engines
260°C		→ gas oil	fuel for diesels
340°C		→ fuel oil	central heating ointments, polishes
		→ bitumen	road surfacing, waterproofing

infractionating column

CRUDE OIL→

heater

(heaviest)

Summary

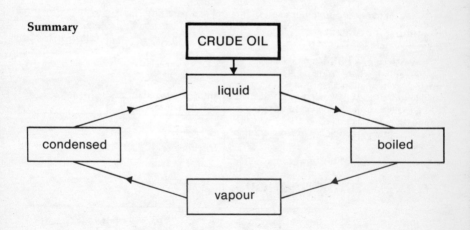

CRUDE OIL → liquid → condensed → vapour → boiled → liquid

Close reading

Chemicals from naphtha and their products

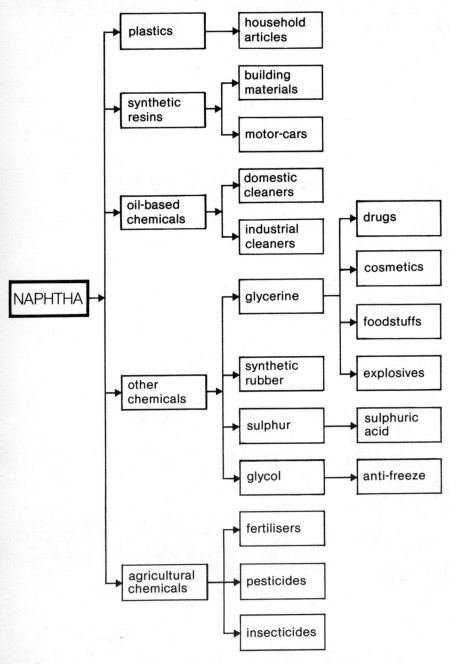

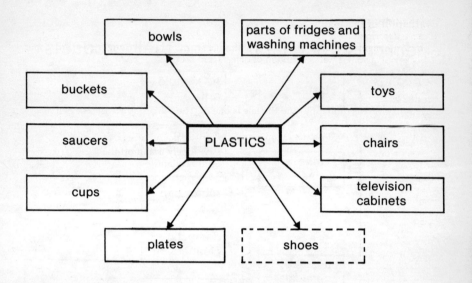

Unit 9 **Literature**

Section A

Cohesion: discourse markers

1 ll. 1–6
2 ll. 7–10
3 ll. 11–12
4 ll. 13–16

5 ll. 17–18
6 ll. 19–24
7 ll. 25–8

Cohesion: reference

a Caxton(s) l. 1
b Caxtons (l. 1)
c the sky (l. 7)
d when the sky is tired of flight and rests its soft machine on ground (ll. 7–8)
e Rain (l. 11)
f a haunted apparatus (l. 19)

Interpretation

1 books (ll. 1–6)   car (ll. 13–16)   watch (l. 17)   clock (l. 18)   telephone (ll. 19–24)
2 crying (l. 3)   laughing (l. 4)   sleeping (ll. 25–6)   dreaming (ll. 27–8)
3 a Mist is described with this metaphor: the sky (clouds), like a space machine, comes down and rests its underside on the ground.

   b Rain has a blurring effect similar to that on a cloudy television screen, either when it is faulty or when the set is between stations so that the screen is a mass of flickering dots. It is darker when it rains, hence colours seen through rain appear darker.

   c The lock and key are the ignition, which starts the car and so 'frees the world for movement'. The film is what can be seen flashing past, through either the wind-screen or side windows.

   d A telephone is seen as something strange that sleeps all the time and snores when you pick it up (this being a reference to the dialling tone). When it rings, it is seen as crying like a baby and needing to be soothed by being talked to (into the receiver). Dialling a number is perceived as 'tickling with a finger'.

Evaluation of the text
1 a a description
  b An imaginary Martian is visiting a strange world and is writing a postcard home, giving a superficial description of objects and actions.

Section B

Prediction
tragedy: Deirdre is 'unhappy' and the tale is one of 'The Three *Sorrows* of Storytelling'.

Scanning
1 Ulster
2 Troubler
3 King Conor
4 A lonely island off the western coast of Scotland

Close reading
1 a bird: 'a raven alighting'/'the raven's wing'
2 a rival
  a heroine
  an elopement
  a death (that of the calf)

Word use: equivalents
killed: slain
ran away: fled
young woman: maiden
landing: alighting
anger: wrath
begged: pleaded
marry: wed
really: truly
They are archaic words, nowadays used only poetically – a suitable style for legends or stories from the past. They have a dramatic narrative effect.

Interpretation
1 Direct speech has a dramatic, poetic quality and its use draws attention to the speaker, in this case Deirdre, who is thus highlighted as the central character. It lends vividness to the story. Further examples are lines 12–14, 15–16, 17–18, 24–5.
2 'hair like the raven's wing, skin like snow, and cheeks as red as blood' (ll. 21–2). Colours represent human qualities, e.g. green=envy, yellow=cowardice. Black, red and white are frequently recurring colours in European legends and fairy stories, e.g. *The Black Knight* (Arthurian legend), *Little Red Riding Hood* (fairy story), *Snow White and the Seven Dwarves* (fairy story).
3 Repetition was a way of ensuring the listener of a narrated story remembered its important elements. Storytelling is an oral tradition, and all stories, knowledge and ideas were related before literacy became widespread. The early Bards (or story-tellers) chanted and sang, as well as speaking, their stories. Repetition is also a feature of songs (the chorus), poetry (ballads) and legends (sagas). Here there is also an element of magic or sorcery (ritual in religion and prophecy) in the repetition of the three colours in the description of Naoise.
4 three brothers
  the King's three daughters/sons
  Historically 3 is a mystical/magical
  the three bears
      number. Further examples are:
  three coins in the fountain
  three wishes
  the Holy Trinity
  three wise men

Anticipation
a curse
a rival
a heroine
a death
a hero

Prediction
1 I FOUND: a No   b Yes   c No   d No   e No   f No   g Yes
2 King Conor became more and more jealous of Naoise and Deirdre and sent a message to them in Scotland saying that if they returned to Ireland they would be safe. But he secretly planned to have them killed when they set foot on Irish soil again. Deirdre had a dream in which she saw three birds with three drops of honey in their beaks which they gave to the three brothers before taking away three drops of their blood. Deirdre

interpreted this as a sign that Conor was not to be trusted 'for sweet are the words of a man who smiles while he meditates on blood and vengeance'. But they are persuaded to return to Ireland by an old friend, sent by Conor, and when they arrive they are captured by Conor.

Interpretation

1 The sword of Manannan, the sea god. Its use indicates the heroic stature of Naoise and his courage. An element of the supernatural or magic was essential to storytelling to show the relationship between heroes and the gods.
2 the reluctance of the Ulstermen to kill the brothers
   the grief of Deirdre
   Deirdre's love for Naoise (she died of a broken heart)
3 lions: these represent fearlessness, strength, courage
   hawks: these represent speed and accuracy in killing
   These noble creatures are likened to the brothers to show they had the same qualities.
   The figure three appears four times.
   The lament serves as an epitaph. It sums up the whole tragedy, the lives of Deirdre and the brothers and the unavoidable fate that awaited them.

Section C

Skimming for content

1 At a bus stop in London
2 Five
3 Two: the woman and, briefly, the lady

Close reading

   a I   b I   c I   d T   e F

Interpretation

1 a Probably in the same way as she asked the second man at the end of the sketch, i.e. flirtatiously.
  b Insultingly
  c Men who prey on women.
  d Prison
  e She equates foreigners with trouble and bad behaviour. In contrast she is an honest woman because she is a local woman.
  f This is meant insultingly. It could be a reference to the woman's class (and thus, by implication, her moneyed status) or job (by implication, a prostitute).
2 a That no one is replying to her. The others at the bus stop are deliberately trying not to get involved with her.
  b Same as a.
  c That she is tired of waiting for a bus or, more likely, of listening to the woman and doesn't want to get involved.

Evaluation of the text

2 a Matter-of-fact
  b To fit the ordinariness of the situation and characters.
  c No. It is about how the British behave in public, both in making advances and in rejecting them, and their inability to communicate easily with strangers.
  d The writer is using humour to expose a situation, to comment upon how people behave in public. The humour is black: on the surface the situation is humorous but underneath we can catch glimpses of desperation (on the part of the woman who speaks) and fear and indifference (on the part of the silent bystanders).

Index

Index